THE WEISER CLASSICS SERIES represents the full range of subjects and genres that have been part of Weiser's publishing program for over sixty years, from tarot, divination, and magick to alchemy and esoteric philosophy. Drawing on Weiser's extensive backlist, the series offers works by renowned authors and spiritual teachers, foundational texts, as well as introductory guides on an array of topics.

———

T0020923

THE HANDBOOK OF
YORUBA
RELIGIOUS CONCEPTS

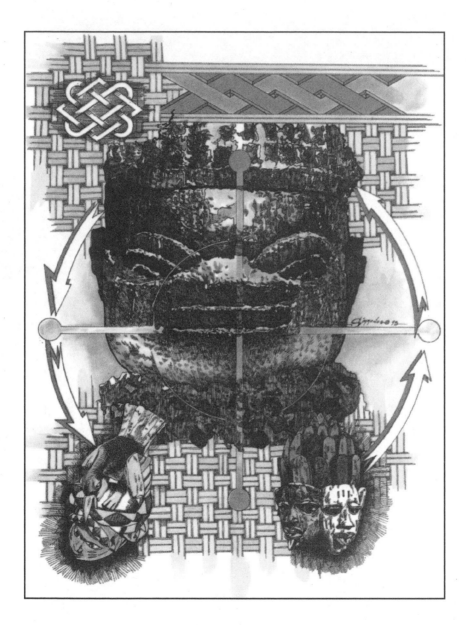

THE HANDBOOK OF

YORUBA RELIGIOUS CONCEPTS

REVISED EDITION

BABA IFA KARADE

WEISER
BOOKS

This edition first published in 2020 by Weiser Books an imprint of
Red Wheel/Weiser, LLC
With offices at:
65 Parker Street, Suite 7
Newburyport, MA 01950
www.redwheelweiser.com

This book describes certain practices that are traditional to Yoruba, including animal
sacrifice. The publisher does not advocate such practices, but as they are a part of
Yoruba belief and ritual, they are represented here.

ISBN: 978-1-57863-667-9
Library of Congress Cataloging-in-Publication Data available upon request.

Cover photograph Full Moon, © Nedelcheva-Williams, Zanara/Sabina
/ Bridgeman Images
Frontispiece: "Adura," by Oswald Simmonds
Typeset in Palatino

Printed in Canada
MAR
5th Printing

Series Editors
Mike Conlon, Production Director, Red Wheel/Weiser
Judika Illes, Editor at Large, Weiser Books
Peter Turner, Associate Publisher, Weiser Books
Kathryn Sky-Peck, Creative Director, Red Wheel/Weiser

CONTENTS

Acknowledgments

To Olodumare, Orunmila, Oriṣa, and Egun.

To the elders of Ile Iya Oloriṣa in Ejigbo, Nigeria, Africa. Special appreciation to Chief Araba Malomo and Iyanla Keye for initiating me into the Yoruba sacerdotal orders of Obatala and Ifa.

To Apetebi Ṣokoya Onayemi Aya Karade for her editing, insight, word processing, illustration, and loving support.

To all my teachers and mentors, including Afolabi Epega of Nigeria, Chique Valdez of Puerto Rico, and Oba Oseijeman Adefunmi I of Oyotunji, South Carolina.

I would also like to personally thank all members/initiates of Ile Tawo Lona (Temple of the Mystic Path) and all who've embraced the Yoruba spiritual/religious tradition.

A Note to the Reader

WHENEVER CULTURES INTERFACE, either through conquest or through peaceful assimilation, the dominant cultural religious structure will extract the more positive aspects of the subjugated culture. What's left in its wake are the negative aspects. People generally accept this negativity because it's the part of the origin or tradition that is presented by the dominant culture. For example, in respect to the Yoruba religious practice, what's left is the negative "voodoo–roots–hoodoo" mentality. This view is devoid of sacred realities born of African thought in respect to religion, philosophy, culture, and dignity. It's becoming quite apparent that the negativity we're subjected to is but a mere shadow of the greatness of a vast and empowering African tradition.

Those seeking their traditional heritage will eventually face the spirituality of their ancestors. When this facing occurs, a deep psychological rift is formed. On one side is the societal dominant religious structure; on the other is the infinite ancestral structure. Adherents to the ancestral Yoruba must be aware of the dangers when crossing the abyss. Spiritual enlightenment, deep study, and gradual acceptance will provide the strength, courage, knowledge, and wisdom necessary to grow, mature, and ultimately transcend.

INTRODUCTION

To REINVESTIGATE THE AFRICAN cultural structure is to reawaken and strengthen the African conceptual consciousness. In respect to religion, concepts are philosophical and transcendental aspects of developmental sciences. They're the fundamental ethos and worldview of a people—of a culture. To be able to conceptualize is one of the higher orders of thinking which inevitably leads a person or people to a greater logic. What's conceived or born from this logic is that oneness with the potential of the Creative Essence brings about oneness in the potential of the human essence. The tenets of Yoruba revolve around this basic concept.

Understandings leading to the acceptance and the actualization of logic in spiritual development are often defined as mystical. The major error of many seekers and adherents of the Yoruba faith is that they confuse mysticism with occultism. "Mystical searching has no relation whatsoever in aim or means to phenomena or powers known as occult. . . . The aim of man's mystical search is to acquire an imperishable consciousness through a progressive communion of his physical body (his temporal reality), with his spiritual being (his immortal reality), and his 'kinship' with his divine cause."[1] It's of the utmost importance that we in this faith strive to understand the way of mystics who set out to harness the energies of existence for the greater good as opposed to those who strive to manipulate those energies to bring about harm, suffering, and discontentment.

Relatedly, basic fundamental concepts of the Yoruba faith have been misinterpreted in the New World. The mysticism of its core has been overshadowed by the occultism of those who extracted and portrayed only the shadow—one present in all religions—that exist.

The aim of the mystic or Yoruba sacerdotal orders isn't to dwell upon occult powers but to seek divine essence and balanced character via the Orişas, the *Odu-Ifa, egun,* and one's *ori.* From a conceptual standpoint, this is all-pervasive and all-important. Seekers or aspirants of the Yoruba religion must be constantly reminded, as reiterated throughout this book, that Yoruba isn't a cult nor is it occult. Yoruba is a divine journey to the inner self and to God-Consciousness. Yoruba is our religion. Yoruba is our existence.

"The indigenous Yoruba has a belief in the existence of a self-existent being who is believed to be responsible for the creation and maintenance of heaven and earth, of men and women, and who also brought into being divinities and spirits who are believed to be functionaries in the theocratic world as well as intermediaries between mankind and the self-existent Being."[2] The Yoruba word for God is both *Olodumare* and *Olorun.* There's no doubt that the Yoruba civilization conceived a One God theosophy eons before external influences brought about by Western invasion, enslavement, and colonialism. The proof is in the sacred Odu-Ifa scriptures once passed down orally and now in written form (much like the Khemetians, Greeks, Romans, Hebrews, Hindus, Native Americans, and other ancient civilizations).

Traditional systems such as Yoruba are seen as being pagan and heathenistic by those of today's proclaimed major world religions and faiths. Clearly, the absurdity of such views is relative to the lack of spiritual and religious substance of those who hold them. To say that one religion is pagan is to say that they're all pagan. Inscribed within the very scriptures of religious cultures throughout the world and throughout time there exist concrete, substantial, and tangible recognition of abstract, insubstantial, intangible manifestations of emotions, mental elucidations and modifications, supernatural beings, transcendental worlds and forces that direct the creation, evolution, and destruction of all things. Rituals, symbolic artistic creations, and sacred physical positions and utterances all demonstrate the human need and ability to make sense of the multiplicity of realities that exist within the universe and, as sentient beings, transcend as a result.

Aspirants are directed to see the Orişas as divinities of the Yoruba cosmology and as emanations of the Olodumare. The Orişas aren't simply mythological constructs designed to satisfy the lower mind and intent of humans. As divinities and angels in religious context they, the Orişas, were created and sent by Olodumare to assist in the spiritual and physical evolution and upliftment of humankind. It's our recognition and our reliance on these elemental beings that have brought about the necessity to make *ebo* and *adimu*: sacrifices and offerings; to have *dafa*: divination; and, most importantly, *alaaşe*: to live in accordance with ancestral guidance.

"In the Judeo-Christian culture, the word for angels signifies their work as messengers, but other words for angels signify their essence. They're called gods, the sons of gods, ministers, servants, watchers, the holy ones. They constitute the court of Heaven."[3] Although the Judeo-Christian emphasis is clear, it should be fully realized that concepts of angels, seraphs, avatars, saints, and holy persons existed long before their arrival. For example, the Yoruba concept of ancestors and Orişas as messengers of Olodumare was in effect thousands of years prior to Judaism and Christianity. Native people throughout the world speak of being shown how to farm and domesticate animals, perform rituals, build temples, etc., by holy messengers best described as gods or demigods. Ancient peoples of all world cultures depict these supernatural beings as seen through cultural eyes. The ancient Yoruba are no different in this respect.

The reality of angelic or dimensional entities is fortified by faith and conviction. In the Yoruba religious system, one must believe in the orişas in order to ascend to God-Consciousness and to reach *eniyan gidi*: the divine state of human being. Yet, a disruption of this endeavor has been brought about by Christian and Islamic influences. Burnham states, "Islamic angels fell after the creation of humans, but Christian angels fell before the creation of the human race."[4] The importance here is that Yoruba orişas never fell in respect to divine grace. There are negating forces—*ajogun* or "demonic spirits"—but there is no Satan or Devil. Resistance to transmuting the orişa Eşu-Elegba into Satan, as an example, must be kept vibrant at any and all cost.

Religious sects that don't hold angelic influences as a major part of divine intervention are apt to downplay and corrupt the spiritual insights of those religious sects that do. (We see this in different doctrines held by Catholics and Protestants.) Aspirants of the Yoruba religion should understand that different basic concepts of cultural and religious structures give rise to great misunderstandings and misdirection primarily held by the dominant society or culture. The supreme purpose of this work is to prevent such from occurring.

THE YORUBA HISTORY

Students or aspirants of any religious system are guided by the knowledge and insights of the teachers of that system. They're educated in the geographical, historical, and political dynamics that have influenced the beginnings and the expansion of their specific religion and those that have played a role in its development. The same holds true for Yoruba aspirants—especially New World descendants. Although aspirants seek religious heritage, as well as ancestral origins, many know little or nothing of the history of Yorubaland in Nigeria, West Africa. I've provided several key points for the purpose of study and contemplation.

As an introduction, let it be stated that the origins of the people and culture known as Yoruba are wrapped in antiquity so that to exactly say where and when it all began is impossible. More research on the topic is needed. And the application of knowledge in the forms of religion, mass media, social media, literature, education, and self-development is viewed as a determined necessity.

The Yoruba history we know begins with the migration of an East African population across the trans-African route leading from the mid-Nile river area to the mid-Niger. Basil Davidson writes, "migrating peoples undoubtedly used this route from times that were exceedingly remote . . . that two thousand years ago and more the climate and vegetation would have treated trans-African travelers in a gentler way than they do now."[1] Davidson continues, "they came this way [the route] from the earliest of times; and their beliefs and their inventions came with them."[2]

Archaeologists, according to M. Omoleya, inform us that the Nigerian region was inhabited more than forty thousand years ago, or as far back as 65,000 B.C.E.[3] This civilization has been deemed, in part, the Nok culture. The Nok culture was visited by the "Yoruba group," between 2000 B.C.E. and 500 B.C.E. The group was led, according to Yoruba historical accounts, by King Oduduwa, who settled somewhat peacefully in the already established Ile-Ife, the sacred city of the indigenous people. The time period was the Bronze Age, indicating that the civilization of both groups was at high levels.

Cheik Anta Diop proclaims, "The Yoruba, during antiquity, lived in ancient Egypt before migrating to the Atlantic coast." He uses as demonstration the similarity or identity of languages, religious beliefs, customs and names of persons, places and things.[4] The key point, or focus, in respect to Yoruba religious evolution is that the Egyptian order coupled with the earlier peoples produced the more defined statement of what makes Yoruba.

In the *History of West Africa A.D. 1000–1800*, Onwubiko states, "According to tradition, Oduduwa, the chief ancestor and first king of the Yoruba settled at Ile-Ife. From this point his descendants became the kings and queens of Yoruba cities and territories."[5] The greatest of Oduduwa's descendants was Oranmiyan who became the Alafin or ruler of the Oyo state somewhere around 1400 C.E. Oranmiyan's armies marched across the Southern Sudan and penetrated deep into the great tropical forest conquering and laying the foundations of the Yoruba Empire. Centuries of spectacular glory and achievement followed the reign of Oranmiyan. It was during this great era that Yoruba people reestablished Ile-Ife as the spiritual capital and Oyo as the governmental seat.

Enslavement of West Africans: An Overview

Onwubiko's research indicates that "the wars of expansion [impacting the Yoruba] during the 16th and 17th centuries were not fought to procure slaves for export to the coast but for local service on Yoruba farms. It was not until the 18th century that wars to provide slaves for sale to Europeans became important."[6]

Enslavement from European hands began in the 15th and 16th centuries. Around 1530, the Portuguese began to transport Africans from the West Coast to Spanish mines and plantations in the New World. Later, other European nations became involved. France, England, Holland, and Spain soon became active in the brutal manipulation and deception that somehow became known as the "slave trade." This era began in 1488 when Bartolomeu Dias sailed from Portugal and around the Cape of Good Hope. In 1498, Vasco da Gama explored the coastal regions of Africa, opening the gates for European exploration and take-over. Both Dias and da Gama were seeking a route to the East Indies and both were taking Africans to Europe in bondage.

When the New World was invaded in 1492, Africans were— after the Europeans failed to fully enslave the Native Americans— forced into chattel bondage and shipped to labor in what was to become the New World: The United States, South America, Central America, and the Caribbean. It must be noted that Africans were also enslaved in Europe during this era.

Islamic jihads also swept through Africa clear to the western coastal regions. This era lasted from the 7th century through the 19th century. The trans-Saharan slave trade flourished. The Yoruba Nation was decimated and depleted of its most natural resource and eventually collapsed as a result of this dual attack on its land (Arabs and Europeans). Arabs basically enslaved Africans on the east coast and central regions. The greater emphasis was on the trade of elephant tusks and other exotic merchandise. The laborers needed to transport the goods were captives of wars and raids.

It's important to note that the largest numbers of Africans enslaved for New World labor came from the Yoruba. It's also important to note that most of those enslaved were war prisoners taken from elite classes of soldiers and warrior priests. Hence, the New World became inundated with a people knowledgeable of their culture and who were initiated members of its higher teachings. It's no small wonder that the Yoruba culture became the dominant theme of African transference to America no matter the hardships and sufferings imposed. This isn't to say that the cultures of other African nations were not as important. The Bini, the Igbo, the Congolese, the people of Ghana and Senegal, and others played a vital role in the blending of Africa into the fabric of the New World, and the Old World as well.

African descendants were transported to New World countries like Cuba, Puerto Rico, Trinidad, Jamaica, Haiti, the Dominican Republic, and other islands of the West Indies; to Brazil, Argentina, Colombia, Venezuela, and other countries of South America; and, finally, to the colonies and emerging states of North America. (As a note: Prior to and during this era, Africans were transported as enslaved humans to England, France, Belgium, the Netherlands, and other European countries.)

The crossing of the Atlantic Ocean to reach the New World has been termed the Middle Passage, the Triangle Trade, and Maafa. It has been estimated that over 75 million captives were taken during the 14th through 18th centuries. This doesn't include the higher numbers enslaved by Arabs or the numbers taken to Europe. The enslavement of Africans remains the greatest atrocity of human history and a crime against humanity.

African people were solidly encased in the religion of their own culture and the zeal to implant it also existed—especially for the Yoruba. Maureen Warner-Lewis, in her book *Guinea's Other Suns*, quotes a study from Mobogunji and Omer-Cooper 1971–1977: "The fact that the Yoruba were dragged into the slave trade in such huge numbers and so soon before the trade was brought to an end had several important consequences. . . . Their culture and religion tended to dominate the sub-culture of the slave society and to submerge and absorb into itself surviving elements of African culture."[7]

There also came into being a type of homogenization or synthesis of the African religions and Christianity. From the African perspective there arose a special Christian interpretation and practice. Warner-Lewis continues, "Some [Africans] denounced the traditional gods; others did not even credit their existence. On the other hand, a large number maintained traditional beliefs and practices alongside Christianity, using one spiritual resource to supplement and complement the other."[8] For a people stripped of fundamental social structures and mores, the concepts of spirit and religion have miraculously survived. Africans, however, maintained the "African" within the imposed and enforced Christianity. Evident is the creation of "Negro" field hollers, spirituals, getting the holy ghost (a form of possession), shouting, speaking in tongues, intense preaching, music, praise dancing, and so forth. The African soul was not extinguished during enslavement, but simply transfigured to meet the Euro-social pressures of chattel slavery, racial prejudice, and near genocidal practices and directives.

Robert Farris Thompson writes in his introduction to *Flash of the Spirit* that "The Yoruba are black Africa's largest population and are creators of one of the premier cultures of the world. The Yoruba believe themselves descended from goddesses and gods, from an ancient spiritual capital, Ile-Ife. They show their special concern for the proprieties of right living through their worship of major goddesses and gods, each essentially a unique manifestation of aṣe . . . only the most widely and important (deities) survived the vicissitudes of the Atlantic Trade."[9]

These important deities bear the name of oriṣas, which are the divinities of Yoruba people. The oriṣas are comprised of Eṣu-Elegba, Obatala, Oṣun, Ogun, Yemoja, Ṣango, Oya, and numerous others. Each requires special worship, song, and sacrifice. The ability to keep these deities alive in the world-reality of the Yoruba led to the conscious masking of them behind Catholic saints and related social-ritual performances. This process is known as syncretism. Catholicism, with its numerous patron saints, made the masking possible. And since the Portuguese and Spanish were Catholic and also major enslavers of Yoruba elite prisoners, the tradition survived virtually intact, at least at the core.

Among the Euro-speaking colonies, religious sects were formed: Santeria in Puerto Rico, Candomble in Brazil, Ṣango Baptise in Trinidad, Vodun in Haiti, and Lucumi/Santeria in Cuba. The European influences, although great, could not deter the African descendants from secretly maintaining their tradition. Even the language of the Yoruba remained somewhat intact, as did cultural mannerisms.

English Protestants were also involved in the slave trade, and they had greater success in "domesticating" the enslaved Africans, hence lessening African culture power as evident when comparing the United States to Cuba or Brazil, which are Catholic based. Lack of numerous patron saints in the religious construct made it difficult to mask the Yoruba religion. Lack of tropical environments in North America also made it difficult for the African to maintain cultural-geographic relativity. Finally, the North American/United States emphasis on inbreeding African slaves and later the internal slave trade brought an end to fresh ideas and religious fervor brought and incited by newly arrived captives. Yet remnants of the Yoruba tradition emerged and flourished as High John the Conqueror, Roots, Voodoo, etc.

Today, many of Africa's descendants are openly embracing the Yoruba faith and practice. Because of political struggles, especially in the 1950s, New World people from the Caribbean found their way to the United States. They were mainly from Cuba, sometimes called "Little Africa." The Cubans brought with them the Yoruba religion and practice as they'd interpreted it. Now, African descendants in the United States and Brazil are stepping beyond the syncretism and its Christian impact and influence and religious interpretations. They're returning to the more unadulterated form of life and ancestral religion known as Yoruba or Ifa. Serious aspirants of this religious/spiritual movement have connected themselves with Nigerian priests and priestesses who now reside in the United States. A few, like myself, have traveled to Nigeria for initiations and insights from the source, or at least closer to it.

The key point realized is that history, no matter how tragic, provides at its end the dissemination of a people and culture throughout the globe. Wars, enslavement, forced migrations, famines, etc., have led to the displacement of millions upon millions of human beings, but we too often see the physical traumas of such shattering and not the cultural impacts made on the world. If history continues to repeat itself, which it most likely will, then we will continue to see the braiding of humanity into a oneness, even if the braiding is painful and forced.

On the other end of this nightmare is the realization that dissemination occurs via peaceful means as well. Books and other forms of literature and study also spread the thoughts and philosophies, and religions of numerous cultures. Art and music add to the humanities that open us to the power of being human. And now, with the advent of the internet and social media the world is but a fingertip or voice command away. Study of the Yoruba religion is no longer held in secret by the enslaved or warped by shifting notions of magic and demonic practices. The potency of its core is available to not only the survivors of its history but to the entire world.

Table 1: A limited comparison of Yoruba oriṣas with the New World survivals of the oriṣa tradition. Although the names are slightly different, the attributes of the oriṣas are fundamentally the same throughout. Other branches, though unmentioned, do exist.

Yoruba: Ifa/Oriṣa	Santeria/ Lucumi: Oriṣa	Candomble: Orixa	Vodou: Iwa/Loa
Eṣu	Eleggua	Exu	Legba
Obatala	Obatala	Oxala	Batala, Blanc Dani
Yemoja	Yemaya	Iemanja	Agwe, La Balianne, Yemalla
Oṣun	Ochun	Oxum	Erzuli
Ogun	Ogun	Ogum	Ogu, Gu, Ogoun
Oshoosi	Ochossi	Oxossi	Age
Osain	Osain	Ossaim	Erinle
Ṣango	Chango	Xango	Xevioso
Oya	Oya	Oya/Iansa	Aieda-Lenso, Olla
Babalu-aye	Babalu-Aye	Omolu/ Babalulye	Sakpata
Olokun	Olokun	Olokun	Agwe, Mami Wata

ORUNMILA AND THE IFA CORPUS

Orunmila is deemed the prophet of the Yoruba religion and culture. It was Orunmila who developed and expounded upon the system of esoteric worship known to this day as Ifa. Through the study of human nature and divine nature, Orunmila saw that dual levels of potentiality existed. Through him we understand that the study of animate and inanimate, manifest and unmanifest, visible and invisible worlds leads to fundamental understandings of cultural ontology and that these fundamental understandings bring about the evolution and transcendence of human spirit, which in turn encourages divine behavior, worldly progression, and expanded cosmology.

Orunmila (not unlike other prophets) became a deified personage who'd been elevated to a central point in the creative origin of life itself. According to the Yoruba religion, Orunmila is said to hold a position comparable to the "son of God." He's also said to have been present (in conscious-divine form) when Olodumare created all beings. Hence, he knows the truth of all beings and, too, the destiny of all beings.

Orunmila is the most esoteric of Yoruba *irunmole*: entities of light. He acts and speaks yet has no physical form. There are no sculptured reflections of Orunmila. All references of him are expressed through the divinatory implements, the ikin and the opele. Those of this sacerdotal order are known as *babalawos* or *iyalawos*: father of mysteries or mother of mysteries, respectively.

Orunmila's physical origins are shrouded in ancient legend. It's believed that he was born of humble West African parents. To the people of the land he was clearly recognized as a divine child, and although poor and crippled he expressed from the onset divine wisdom and attributes. Orunmila grew to be known as "the little man with the big head." His great intelligence super-seded all known teachings and his divine nature was seen as a blessing of the oriṣas.

As Orunmila matured he traveled across the continent of Africa sharing wisdom with the prophets and sages of the land. There's evidence of Orunmila's influence in ancient Khemet (Egypt) and in pre-Christian era Judaism. Yet, the potency of Orunmila's teachings were directed to the Yoruba people centered around the city of Ile-Ife. It was here that Orunmila built his temple on Oke Tase, the Sacred Hill. It was here in Ile-Ife that Orunmila gained heavenly status. His name means "Only Heaven knows the way to salvation." Clearly, this indicates his prophetic and messianic status among his followers.

According to oral tradition, Orunmila is described as a Yoruba man who came to Ile-Ife in order to teach a system of ethics, religious belief, and mystic vision. It must be reinforced, however, that Orunmila merely assessed and delivered systems of conscious evolution by means of life study, ritual, and spiritual beliefs that existed eons before his birth. The elders maintain that Ifa is the original religion, and by Orunmila's efforts and travels the religion advanced.

Orunmila, in this sense, isn't seen as the creator of the Yoruba religion, per se (as compared to Abrahamic religions, wherein the prophets are seen as the progenitors of the actual religion, or as in Buddhism). Orunmila is viewed as the structural originator of Ifa's transference to humankind. His name, as aforementioned, is the composite of *Orun lo mo eni ti yio la:* Only Heaven/divine consciousness knows the way of salvation. He is said to be Ibikeji Olodumare (God's second-in-command). Orunmila is the focal point of ancient religious practice. The exact time frame of his presence on earth is difficult to determine though said to be circa 2000 B.C.E.

The teachings of Orunmila provide religious aspirants with the means and potential to reach what's called in Yoruba tradition *titete* (alignment). By studying the Ifa corpus—the once oral scriptures passed from one generation to the next—devotees strive to reach a state of divine oneness. This oneness comes about when one's *ori* (earthly consciousness) is developed and elevated to the place of unification with one's *iponri* (heavenly consciousness).

Orunmila also teaches that such an endeavor is arduous and takes years of soul-searching and effort. Those who embark on an *irin ajo* (spiritual journey) need to do so with a focused mind, a pure heart, and with deep sincerity, for although the attainment is glorious, the pitfalls are horribly devastating. Wisdom, ritual, and transcendence are the key elements of Orunmila's teachings, and they're bound by African cultural interpretation. There's no difference here in light of all world religions.

Ayanmo (destiny), from a religious point of view, describes a person's return to the inner realization of primal essence or divine being. Orunmila proclaimed that humans must return to their divine nature or state of being, that our destiny is to reach or return to our divine state internally and heavenly, and that each of us is to live upon the earth plane existence as a reflection of that divine state. This is the supreme reason for true Ifa religious involvement.

Orunmila continues in his religious corpus known as Ifa that one's destiny can be reached through:

a.   The divinatory processes left to us by the ancestors

b.   Prescriptions of ritual and sacrifice to the spiritual dimensional beings whose forces impact upon human development and evolution

c.   The moral ethics that humans must adhere to in order to be victorious over oppressive human acts and malevolent spirits

The ancients, or elders, who are the Ifa corpus embodied are known in total as the Odu. The Odu are comprised of sixteen heavenly prophets who existed when the earth was very young. Sent to earth by the *Ara Orun* (heavenly council), they imparted their divine essence and prophesized. They relied on both *Orun* (heavenly) and *Aye* (earthly life experiences) so as to relate to and then elevate the consciousness of the people. These sixteen ancients revealed themselves to Orunmila and are now said to be his heavenly disciples from a timeless cosmic eternity. Yet the name Odu comes from the name of one of Orunmila's wives. In Ifa, women play a different role than in Western religions: Women aren't the cause of sin or the separation of humans from God!

Each of the Odu represents the epitome of Yoruba proverbial wisdom and religiosity. Each contains an enormous amount of *ese*: verses and *kiki* (moral teachings) expressed through the *itan* (mythological, historical, and social development). The priests and priestesses of Yoruba are set to learn and apply the knowledge and ancient wisdom of the Odu so as to present ways of transcendence and salvation to spiritual seekers. Each of the *Oju Odu* or *Olodu* (sixteen major Odu) and the *Omo Odu* or *Amulu* (240 minor Odu) is said to contain 1,680 verses, or moral codes, making such an endeavor a great one. And although no one is said to

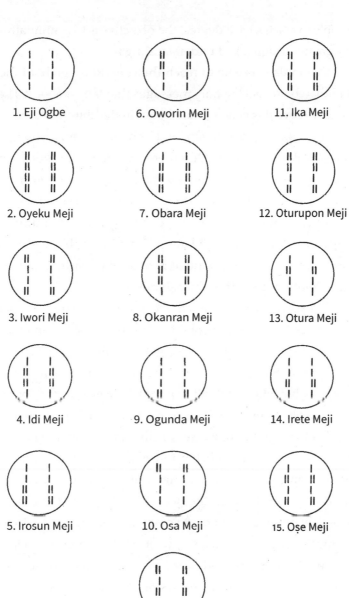

Figure 1. The sixteen major Odu (Oju Odu) and their patterns.

be able to reach such a degree, the objective is to continually strive for greater insights and understandings.

Orunmila was able to reach the conscious height of the Odu and thereby reveal the holy messages that they embody. The ability to achieve this state is manifested in the ability to divine. Each Odu has its own mark pattern and its own accounts, rituals, ethics, and morals. Within each Odu there exist revelations of the divine and oppressive forces known as *ajagun* and *ajogun,* respectively. The orişas are manifestations of heaven sent to continually wrestle with the human nature in order to uplift it—to purify it. The ajogun are the "demonic" beings. They're earthly and heavenly forces whose destructive intent is to keep us earthbound, waylay our evolution, and offset our salvation.

To experience divination in the Yoruba context is to experience the core essence of Yoruba philosophy and worship. Unfortunately, divination is too often related to "getting a reading," which, according to some, belittles and berates the sacred act. Psychics can "read" a person, but religiosity isn't required. However, a sense of religiosity must be present when *dafa* or Ifa divination is performed.

It's through the processes of divination that seekers come to know of themselves and the forces that are shaping their past, present, and future lives. Through the process of divination, seekers come to understand the need for alignment with their most heavenly of selves and how to overcome the opposing forces that disrupt all efforts. Study, interpretation, reflection, and refinement of the psychological and spiritual dimensions are foremost as novices undertake the austerities of Orunmila's teachings.

Figure 1 depicts the sixteen Odu patterns as distinguished by marks of (I) for light/open and (II) for dark/closed. In Table 2 (see page 18), the Odu are represented along with one of the verses. Other world religious teachings are added by way of comparative analysis so that the *ologberi* (uninitiated) and the *aborişas* (initiated) and the o'lorisas (priests/priestesses) novices won't be constricted in their thinking. It must be constantly reinforced that Yoruba is of a religious world order. Plus, the revelations of Orunmila need to be open to all. As a note, the order of the Odu isn't carved in stone. For example, we find changes based on regions within West Africa. We also see a different order when the o'lorisas, the priestly of the orisas, use the obi or cowrie shells to divine. However, though the orders may vary, the core content of the Odu remains consistent. As a note: The orisa priests/priestesses cast the cowrie shells twice to get a double Odu; the ikin twice beat by the Ifa priests also produces a double Odu. The opele of Ifa show a double-side read from left to right when cast. For example, a divination may come doubled, and that is called Odu Meji. When not doubled, it's called by the first cast, then the second, or Omo Odu—for example, Oworin Idi, Ogbe Osa, Irosun Oworin. The Omo Odu have their own verses and content, as well.

What's profoundly interesting is that once the Odu has been determined the questions of *ire* (blessings) or *ibi* (curses) are then asked and by due process answered. For example, the Odu may state its content, but the next step is to determine if it comes with ire or ibi. Ire could come from the orisa and/or the ancestors and/ or Ifa, the husband and/or the wife, the mother and/or father, the ori and/or endeavors, the priest/priestess and/or spiritualist and/or physician, and so on. Ibi could come from sickness and/ or death, loss and/or paralysis, trouble and/or curses, imprisonment and/or afflictions, etc. The point here is that Ifa—unlike many world religions—sees the essence of those the devotee interacts with and is affected by and how it leads to the betterment or detriment of the devotee's character, worldly progression, and, ultimately, heavenly salvation. Offerings and/or sacrifices are then made to the respective *ajagun* (divinities) and/or *ajogun* (demonic forces) within the Odu.

Table 2. The sixteen major Odu (Oju Odu) and their corresponding religious paths.

Path	Eji Ogbe
Ifa	Those who attain blessings are those who live by their wisdom; only fools know not how to direct their lives. If we do not bear suffering that will fill a basket, we will not receive blessings that will fill a cup. Act not in heat nor haste for you may miss the good things that come in the evening of life.
Biblical	The integrity of the upright shall guide them, but the perverseness of the transgressors shall destroy them. (Proverbs 11:3)
Asian	The superior person is quiet and calm, awaiting the appointments of Heaven. The common person walks in dangerous paths looking for lucky occurrences. (Doctrine of the Mean)
Qur'an	Oh, my son! Establish regular prayer, enjoin what is just, and forbid what is wrong. And bear with patient constancy what'er betide thee; for this is firmness (of purpose) in (the conduct of) affairs. (Sura 31:17)
The Husia (Ancient Egypt)	Those who are blameless in matters of conduct, no words can prevail against them. And those who are self-mastered, the harsh are kinder to them than their own mothers; and all people become their servants. Let your name go forth, then while you yourself are silent you will be recognized and respected. (Kagemni)
African Proverb	The heart of the wise lay quiet like the peaceful waters. (Cameroon)

Path	Oyeku Meji
Ifa	The prevalence of temper outburst and cursing are the causes of difficulty in one's life.
Biblical	Who so diggeth a pit shall fall therein; and he that rolleth a stone, it will return upon him. (Proverbs 26:27) Who so causeth the righteous to go astray in an evil way, he shall fall himself into his own pit; but the upright shall have good things in possession. (Proverbs 28:10)
Qur'an	For God loveth not the arrogant, the vainglorious, (nor) those who are vile or enjoin vileness on others . . . for we have prepared for those who resist faith, a punishment that steeps them to contempt. (Sura 4:36, 37)
African Proverb	Ashes fly back into the face of he who throws them. (Niger)

Path	Iwori Meji
Ifa	Your children will be raised under much hardship. However, you should continuously persevere in respect to their correct upbringing.
Biblical	Train up a child in the way they should go; and when they are old they will not depart from it (the training). (Proverbs 22:6)
Asian	Teach your sons (children) so that the straightforward may yet be mild, the gentle may yet be dignified, the strong not tyrannical, and the impetuous not arrogant. (Menicus)
Kemet (Ancient Egypt)	If you are parents of worth and wisdom, train your children so that they may be pleasing to God . . . but if they fail to follow your course, oppose your will, reject all counsel, and set their mouth in motion with vile words, then drive them away. (Ptah-Hotep)

Path	Edi Meji
Ifa	It is a grave tragedy to die young so we pray, "May we be sufficiently ripe before we are eaten up by death; and we seek by all means to attain long life."
Biblical	The fear of the Lord prolongeth days; but the years of the wicked shall be shortened. (Proverbs 10:27) Be not righteous over much; neither make thyself over wise. Why shouldest thou destroy thyself? Be not over much wicked, neither be thou foolish; why shouldest thou die before thy time? (Ecclesiastes 7:16–17)

Path	Irosun Meji
Ifa	Seek the place of honor, respect, and accomplishment in this world; for you will become a revered ancestor.
The Husia (Ancient Egypt)	Every person teaches as they act. They will speak to the children so that they will speak to their children. Each person will set an example and not give offense. (Ptah-Hotep) Follow the footsteps of your ancestors, for the mind is trained through knowledge. Behold their words, endure in books. (Kheti) Pour libations for your father and mother who rest in the valley of the dead. God will witness your action and accept it . . . for as you do for your parents, your children will do for you also. (Ani)

Path	Oworin Meji
Ifa	To be told and to like it; to be given advice and to accept it; to take advice in order to know what the world is like.
Biblical	Hear counsel and receive instruction that thou mayest be wise in the latter end. (Proverbs 19:20)
African Proverb	Give them advice and counsel them; if they do not learn, let adversity teach them. (Ethiopia)

Path	Obara Meji
Ifa	One must be uplifted from poverty-stricken acceptance and state of mind. There is no virtue in being in poverty. Be industrious and accomplish your desires. Wealth will come.
Biblical	Love not sleep, lest thou come to poverty; open thine eyes, and thou shalt be satisfied with bread. (Proverbs 20:13)
The Husia (Ancient Egypt)	Be diligent as long as you live, always doing more than is commanded of you. Do not misuse your time while following the heart, for it is offensive to the soul to waste one's time. Do not lose the daily opportunity to increase that which you have. (Ptah-Hotep)
African Proverb	Poverty is slavery. (Somalia)

Path	Okanran Meji
Ifa	One must come to realize that stubbornness is not beneficial; that the truth regarding oneself must be listened to. Do not be overly influenced by your self-defensive ego. Problems in life are caused by negligence of one's self.
Biblical	Every way of a man is right in his own eyes; but the Lord pondereth the hearts. (Proverbs 21:2)
Asian	In archery we have something of the superior person. When the archer misses the center of the target, he turns around and seeks the cause of his failure in himself. (Doctrine of the Mean)
The Husia (Ancient Egypt)	Guard against words and deeds of deception and against words that aren't true. Destroy the desire to do and speak evil within you, for the evil person hath no rest. (Ani)

Path	Ogunda Meji
Ifa	Anger does not do anything for anyone; patience is the father of good character; those who develop patience will enjoy long life.
The Husia (Ancient Egypt)	Be gentle and patient, then your character will be beautiful. It is in the development of character that instruction succeeds. Learn the structure and functioning of the Sky. Learn the structure and functioning of the earth. (Ankhsheshonqi)
African Proverb	A little subtleness is better than a lot of force. (Zaire)

Path	Osa Meji
Ifa	One must cease leading themselves to misfortune. One must cease bringing harm upon themselves.
The Husia (Ancient Egypt)	Gentleness of conduct of every kind causes the wise to be praised. Do not make your mouth harsh or speak loudly with your tongue. For a loud voice does damage to members of the body just like an illness. Do not be so impatient when you ask that you get angry while you are listening. . . . Do not yield often to your tongue in order to advise when you have not been asked. (Phebhor)

Path	Ika Meji
Ifa	It is to be that Ifa divination be continually performed so that the forces in one's life be understood and controlled.
Biblical	Yea, though I walk through the valley of the shadow of death, I will fear no evil. For thou art with me; thy rod and staff thy comfort me. (Psalms 23:4)
Asian	Those who are skillful in managing life entrusted to them may travel on the land without fear . . . for within there is no place of death. (Lao Tzu)

Path	Oturupon Meji
Ifa	The orişa state that we must never raise problems or incite conflict. That we must take the time to be sure of our words even before we speak.
Biblical	A soft answer turneth away wrath; but grievous words stir up anger. (Proverbs 15:1) The tongue of the wise useth knowledge aright; but the mouths of fools poureth out foolishness. (Proverbs 15:2)
Qur'an	And be moderate in thy pace and lower thy voice; for the harshest of sounds without doubt is the braying of the ass. (Sura 31:19)
The Husia (Ancient Egypt)	Offensive words that come from your mouth, if repeated, can make bitter enemies. A person may be ruined by his or her tongue. Take care and you will fare well . . . a harsh answer provokes strife, but one who speaks with gentleness is loved. (Ani)
African Proverb	Do not say the first thing that comes to your mind. (Guinea) If your mouth turns into a knife, it will cut off your lips. (Zimbabwe)

Path	Otura Meji
Ifa	No matter how powerful wickedness is, righteousness overcomes it in the end. The power of falsehood is transient and ephemeral; truth although seemingly slow and weak overcomes falsehood in the end.
Biblical	The eye of the truth shall be established forever; but a lying tongue is but for a moment. (Proverbs 12:19)
Asian	Though the white gem be cast into the dirt, its purity cannot long be sullied; though the good man live in a vile place, his heart cannot be depraved. As the fir and the cypress withstand the rigors of winter, so resplendent wisdom is safe in situations of difficulty and danger. (Wisdom of Kung Fu)
African Proverb	The truth is like gold: keep it locked up and you will find it exactly as you first put it away. (Senegal)

Path	Irete Meji
Ifa	Guard against selfishness; those who are selfish will come to bear their burdens alone.
Biblical	Who stoppeth his ears at the crying of the poor, he also shall cry himself, but shall not be heard. (Proverbs 21:13)
Qur'an	Those who (in charity) spend of their goods by night and by day, in secret and in public, have their reward with their lord. On them shall be no fear, nor shall they grieve. (Sura 2:274)
The Husia (Ancient Egypt)	Help your friends with things you have, for you have these things by the grace of God. If you fail to help your friends, one will say you have a selfish Ka. (Ptah-Hotep) Eat not bread while another stands by hungry without extending your hand to him or her. As for food, it is always here, it is a man or a woman who do not remain . . . one who was rich last year may be vagrant this year. Therefore, be not anxious to fill your belly without regards for others. (Ani)

Path	Oṣe Meji
Ifa	Unless we resort to caution and discretion, we will miss the blessings of prosperity.
Biblical	Wrath is cruel, and anger is outrageous; but who is able to stand before envy. (Proverbs 27:4)
Asian	You may do good without thinking about fame, but fame will come to you nevertheless. You may have fame without aiming at riches, but riches are sure to follow in its wake. You may be rich without wishing to provoke emulation and strife, yet emulation and strife will certainly result. Hence, the superior persons are very cautious about how they do good. (Lieh Tzu)

Path	Ofun Meji
Ifa	Do not speak of those who are ill of mind or crippled of body. Do not leave your home and speak badly of those in trouble.
Biblical	Whoso mocketh the poor (and crippled) reproacheth his maker; and he that is glad at calamities shall not be unpunished. (Proverbs 17:5)
The Husia (Ancient Egypt)	Laugh not at the blind, nor make fun of the dwarf, nor interfere with the plans of the lame. Do not harass those who are in the hands of God, if they err. Surely, humans are clay and straw, and God is the builder. (Amenomope)

THE ORIṢA

The Yoruba contend that the study of nature is foremost. Nature is viewed as the manifestation of Olodumare (also called Edumare), or God through infinite degrees of material and spiritual substance. That essence, translated as aṣe, is the inherent force of all creation. The emphasis of such study or worship isn't centered on the physical object or tangible (as often implied or alluded to), but on the life force and energy and consciousness that bring about its form. The tangible object is but a symbol of the eternal existence that bore it. Olodumare is also called Oba atayese (the Lord who corrects wrongs on earth), Oba ada eda (the Creator of all beings), Olorun (Owner of Heaven), Eledaa (Creator), and Elemii (Owner of the breath of life).

Olodumare, or Edumare, is in all things as the aṣe is the primal essence of all things. It's not the tree, the rock, the statue that African ancestors revere and worship, but the deep energy that brought about its being and what that object specifically refers to on a cultural-historical belief reality. In maintaining this nature religion that is both polytheistic and animistic, the ancestors were able to keep and also strengthen the very real connection between all things and human beings as a part of all things. Yet, there is a God in the Yoruba religious tradition. After worship is completed, we say, *Ki Olodumare gba e o* (May Olodumare accept it).

This concept is basic and fundamental in respect to religious involvement. Olodumare, the Creator, must be seen in all things and recognized among devotees as core to the Yoruba faith. Humans, devoid of oppressive ego, must see themselves as also part of Olodumare's creation and behave accordingly. In respect to the orisa, it's to be understood that as divinities or avatars or supernatural forces they, too, are a part of the universal essence and energy—spirit. And they're comprised of greater heavenly properties and are closer to the source of Existence. Their ability to act on behalf of human beings is generally stated as divine intervention. Such intervention is brought about by divination, belief, faith, prayer, song, offerings, sacrifice, and praise.

Orisa as a term is actually the combination of two Yoruba words: *ori,* the reflective spark of human consciousness embedded in human essence, and *sha,* the ultimate potentiality of that consciousness to enter into or assimilate itself into the divine consciousness. There's said to be 400 + 1 orisas in the Yoruba cosmology. The +1 is a statement of infinite additions or possibilities.

The human consciousness needs to pass through stages of development in order to attain the highest levels. The orisas symbolize the forces and forms of human divinity potential. In *Her Bak,* it's written that, "the Neters [divine beings, avatars, orisas] are an expression of the principles and functions of divine power manifesting in nature. Their names and images as pictured in the myths define such principles and functions and they are offered that the student may learn to know them and seek them in him/herself."[1] This concept maintained by the ancients of Egypt and throughout Africa is evident, though somewhat dismissed, in all forms of religious and spiritual development.

"The Yoruba maintain that worship of the orisas assist in the development of *iwa-pele* or balanced character and balanced attitude. That the most important purpose of a person on earth is to come and exhibit that character and attitude."[2] Religion, as a custom of worship, is not man's purpose, but only a means to an end while the end itself is iwa-pele. Thus, the fundamental reality in respect to the divinity of self and the heavenly forces is that of pure and enlightened character development. This is the premise of true orisa involvement. The connection between one's *ori* (consciousness) and *iwa-pele* (behavior) is clearly seen as reciprocal and relative. That is, the more enlightened one's consciousness becomes, in respect to the divine, the more one's behavior reflects the divine. Thus, the individual is deemed saintly or priestly in their development and endeavors.

THE ORISA

Ori

G. Okemyiwa and A. Fubunmi state, "the word *Ori* has many meanings. [Literally] Ori means head. It means the apex of all things, the highest of any endeavor. . . . In the human body Ori is divided into two—the physical head and the spiritual head. . . . The spiritual head is [also] subdivided into two parts: the *Ori Apari* (the internal spiritual Ori) and the *Ori Apere* (the sign of an individual's personal god/orisa)."[3] The Ori Ode (physical head), the Ori Inu (the internal spirit), and the Iponri (the soul space of the inner self) are more noted definitions of the Ori. It's revealed in the Odu: Ogunda Meji that "no god can bless a person without consent of that person's Ori. One whose Ori has accepted the sacrifice is one who should rejoice exceedingly." Sacrifices and/or offerings are first placed at the forehead or top of the devotee's head so that their Ori is appeased.

Esu-Elegba

Esu, as a divinity, is viewed primarily as the powerful holder of the ase or creative potency of the other orisas. For this reason, all sacrifices and offerings must be shared with Esu in some manner. He's the messenger divinity who delivers sacrifices to the orisa from humans and from one orisa to another. Esu holds a conflictual position among humans and orisa alike, for he's the one who "tries their souls." Esu tempts, thwarts, and disrupts. If all tests are passed, he recreates and resurrects. It's because Esu isn't discriminating when it comes to enforcing the laws of being—punishing or rewarding, as the case may be—that he's so respected and revered. He's in close proximity to all forces—positive and negative alike—as he's the prime negotiator between them. Awolalu writes, "The Yoruba tradition holds that Eṣu maintains relationships with the super-sensible world and with human beings on earth. With regard to the super-sensible world, he maintains close relationship with Orunmila who is notable for his wisdom and who knows the wishes of the Deity and the divinities."[4]

It's interesting to note that in Yorubaland, as stated by Awolalu, "Eṣu has no regular priesthood because he's associated with all the other divinities. But, whenever these other divinities are worshipped, due homage is paid to him."[5] Images of Eṣu (generally constructed of clay, wood, stone, or concrete and adorned with cowrie shells) are found in every Yoruba home regardless of the priestly order hierarchy or status of the family. Also, Eṣu is to be propitiated not only first before oriṣa, but also before *Egun* (ancestors). Even babalawos must have a deep and abiding relationship with Eṣu, because it's Eṣu who carries the messages of Ifa.

Obatala

"Obatala, also known as Oriṣa-nla, Oriṣaala, and Ogiyan is deemed the arch-divinity of Yorubaland. Obatala represents the idea of ritual purity and ethical purity symbolized by immaculate whiteness of cloth associated with him. The inside walls of his temples are washed white, his emblems are kept in white containers, and white robes, ornaments, and beads are for his priests and priestesses."[6] Obatala is viewed as the most intelligent and even-tempered of the oriṣas. Not only is he the "father of the oriṣas," but he's also the molder of human form on earth. He's the creative sculptor that forms the embryonic body of infants inside the womb. It was Obatala who first formed humankind out of the earth's clay. Obatala is Olodumare's prime emissary on earth. The followers of Obatala and others appeal to him for children, prosperity, the avenging of wrongs, and the curing of illnesses and deformities. They bring prayers and offerings to his priests, who then present the offerings to the altars and/or shrines on behalf of the followers, and make supplications to Obatala with prayer, acts and behaviors, and meditations.

Oşun

Oşun is the orişa of unconditional love, receptivity, and diplomacy. She's known for her sensuality, fine artistic development, and beauty. Oşun is a river divinity symbolizing clarity and flowing motion. She has powers to heal with cool water and to divine based on her dream revelations and sensual perception. Oşun is said to have many sides. On the one hand she can be very short-tempered and irritable; on the other, she can be calm and fluid. Either could be the case depending on the devotee and/or the nature of the situation.

Oşun is also the divinity of fertility and feminine essence. Women appeal to her for childbearing and for the alleviation of female disorders. She's fond of babies and sought if a baby becomes ill. Oşun is reflected in brass, gold, and shining gems. She's known for her love of honey. Oşun is the orişa of the humanities and fine arts.

Ogun

Ogun is the divinity of iron and all that iron becomes. He's the patron of blacksmiths, hunters, and warriors. Ogun is also the divinity of clearing paths, specifically in respect to building civilizations. He's also depicted as the divinity of mechanization. Ogun is the essence of divine justice and truth on earth. Devotees swear upon him in solemn reverence. He's known for his keen insight into the hearts of men. He's the liberator and executioner in the world.

Yemoja

Yemoja is the divinity of all the oceans. She's said to be the mother of all orişas and expresses her mothering throughout the earthly and heavenly realms. Yemoja is the matriarchal head of the cosmic universe. She's the amniotic fluid in the womb of the pregnant woman, as well as the breasts that nurture. She's known to be very stern and temperamental and expresses the protective energies of the feminine force. Being of the earth essence, she's proficient in the secret arts and will use them to protect her devotees.

Oya

Oya is the divinity that guards the cemetery. More specifically she protects the souls of the departed as they journey onward. Oya is viewed as a warrior with great strength. She stands well on her own but is usually in the company of her counterpart Şango. Oya is recognized for her psychic abilities that manifest in the winds. She's the deity of the storm and hurricanes. Oya is often seen as the deity of death, but upon deeper realization, she's the deity of rebirth, as things must die so that new beginnings arise.

Şango

Şango is the deified *Alafin* (ruler) of medieval Oyo said to have hung himself because of his overindulgence. His elevation to the orişa realm was brought about by his devout followers. They merged him with the deity of lightning and fierce retribution known as Jakuta. Şango's symbol is the double ax mounted on the head of the holy statues or dance wands (Oşe Şango). Şango is the orişa of the drum and dance. He possesses the ability to transform base substance into that which is pure and valuable. His devotees approach him for legal problems, protection from enemies, and to make bad situations better. Often viewed as a bit earthy, Ṣango is revered and earnestly listened to for he speaks only once and is prone to be temperamental.

◊ ◊ ◊

"In Africa, it is believed that divinities or gods are personifications of God's activities and manifestations. God's activities and manifestations are also discernible in natural phenomenon and objects, nature spirits, deified heroes and mythological figures."[7] As the study of oriṣas intensifies, it becomes apparent that nature is a vehicle to god-consciousness. The oriṣas were, according to the Yoruba belief, sent by Olodumare to harness the forces of the molten earth and set evolution into motion. Ogun created the iron chain they descended on. Obatala formed the physical bodies from clay. Their place of arrival was *Oke Ara*: the Hill of Wonder.

The oriṣas are examined in Tables 3, 4, and 5 on the following pages. The depictions show concise views of those attributes most generally related to by New World practitioners. The general notion is that this is where the involvement with oriṣas stops. Aspirants who proclaim their affiliations based on worldly intentions must guard against delusion. Delusion leads to witchcraft or the manipulation of the aṣe in order to satisfy the lower-base self. As devotees study the oriṣas, they must remain true to the major objectives of Yoruba faith—to express *iwa-pele* (divine character, intent, and attitude). Devotees aren't to rest on preconceived notions as to what the oriṣas are about and attempt to "act like" the oriṣa. The goal of Yoruba involvement is clearly stated by Orunmila, the prophet: *Iwa-pele* (divine and balanced character), *Iwa-l'ewa* (oneness with all things), and *Iwa-l'aiye* (righteous living without regression). The culmination of these principles in one's life results in becoming an *eniyan gidi* (transcendental human). In addition, the devotees of Ifa/Yoruba are to work earnestly and tirelessly to advance the world to a state of transformed goodness or *Ipo Rere*.

The orișas—as messengers, helpers, and patrons—"act through" the devotee for the sole purpose of the devotee's transformation, purification, and enlightenment. The așe of the orișas is channeled by the devotee through a process known as *aba*. When an orișa "mounts" the devotee, various characteristics of that orișa are manifested and the "horse" is seen as a divine incarnation of the orișa and respected as such. As Yoruba initiates expand their awareness, more orișas are revealed and the deepness of the orișas are embraced on ever-increasing levels.

Several other orișas along with their attributes are provided below:

Olokun: Orișa of the depths of the ocean.

Oshoosi: Orișa of warriors and hunters.

Ọșun: The staff of the babalawo symbolizing health, wisdom, and protection.

Ibeji: Twins symbolizing the dual aspect of the cosmos.

Oba: River orișa. Goddess of the home.

Aganyu: Orișa of the volcano and core of the earth.

Oko: Orișa of the farm.

Erinle: Orișa of medicine.

Osain: Orișa of plants and herbs.

Babaluaiye: Orișa of sickness and epidemics.

Table 3. The seven major oriṣas and their attributes.

Oriṣa	Attributes
Obatala	Creator of Human Form, Elder of the Oriṣa, Wisdom, Purity, Morality, Strategy, High Intelligence, Peacemaker, Father, God of the White Cloth, Silver.
Elegba	Messenger of the Oriṣa, Courier of Offerings and Sacrifices, Policeman of the Yoruba Cosmology, Guardian of the Crossroads, Holder of Aṣe (Power) among the Oriṣa, Laterite Sone.
Ogun	Oriṣa of Iron, War, Creator of Civilizations, Courage, Strength, Justice and Oaths, Executioner, Path Maker, Force, Stabilization, Security, Protection, Vehicles and Tools.
Yemoja	Motherhood, Mother of Waters, Family, Sexuality, Sorcery, Primal Waters, Nurturer.
Oṣun	Sensuality, Fine Arts and Humanities, Love, Beauty, Graciousness, Gracefulness, Money, Sorcery, Luxury, Brass, God, Cowrie, Rivers, Intuition, Divination.
Ṣango	Kingly, Stately, Orator, Sorcery, Virility, Dance, Music (Drums), Masculinity, Business, Fire, Lightning, Stones, Protector/Warrior, Magnetism.
Oya	Tempest, Guardian of the Cemetery, Winds of Change, Warrior, Hurricanes, Storms, Death, Progression.

Table 4. Correspondences of the orişas with their color, number, and natural environment.

Orişa	Color	Number*	Natural Environment
Obatala	White	8, 24	Mountains, Woods
Elegba	Red and Black White and Black	1, 3, 21	Woods, Crossroads, Gateways
Yemoja	Blue and Crystal	7	Oceans, Lakes (Salt Water)
Oşun	Yellow	5	Rivers, Lakes (Fresh Water)
Ogun	Green and Black	3	Railroads, Woods, Forges
Şango	Red	6, 12	Places Struck by Lightning, Base of Trees
Oya	Reddish-Brown, Rust, Earth Tones	9	Cemetery, Places Hit by Hurricanes, Storms

* Numbers of the orişa may also include their multiples. Colors may be taken in shades.

Table 5. Physiological correspondences.

Orişa	Physical Correspondences
Obatala	Brain, Bones, White Fluids of the Body
Elegba	Sympathetic Nervous System, Parasympathetic Nervous System
Yemoja	Womb, Liver, Breasts, Buttocks
Oşun	Circulatory System, Digestive Organs, Elimination System, Pubic Area
Ogun	Heart, Kidneys (Adrenal Glands), Tendons, and Sinews
Şango	Reproductive System, Bone Marrow, Life Force or Chi
Oya	Lungs, Bronchial Passages, Mucous Membranes

Ewe

The use of *ewe* (medicinal herbs and plants) is an area of great emphasis in this faith. Herbs are used for healing and spiritually empowering purposes. In Yorubaland, herbs are gathered by the priestly and/or by the various types of herbalists who inhabit the regions. The herbs are often made available to the population either through private practice or in a marketplace. In the New World, aspirants are also herbal directed.

Various botanicas (base word *botany*) exist in major cities in the Americas. Here, the priestly and devotees alike go to obtain herbs for baths, religious artifacts, readings, drinking, and so forth. Most botanicas are run by Latinos and some by Haitians, but neither is limited in respect to patronage. Nigerians and people from other African countries have begun to set up businesses in increasing numbers on a global scale. Then, there's the dissemination of information and materials via the internet and social media.

The ewe are for the "healing of nations," and various health food stores provide them in both leaf and capsule form. Adherents to traditional practices are advised to apply herbs before going to synthetic products for healing. Numerous books on herbology can be found. Exploration of the possibilities of herbal use is recommended.

Table 6 provides examples of the ewe based on the presiding orişa correspondence. It's best that novices seek out divination before attempting to get and prepare herbal solutions. It's also advisable to rely on priests and herbalists to begin the healing process before getting involved with the properties and powers of herbs yourself.

Table 6. The ewe and presiding oriṣa.

Oriṣa	Ewe for Medicinal Usage
Obatala	Skullcap, Sage, Kola Nut, Basil, Hyssop, Blue Vervain, White Willow, Valerian
Elegba	All Herbs
Oṣun	Yellow Dock, Burdock, Cinnamon, Damiana, Anis, Raspberry, Yarrow, Chamomile, Lotus, Jasmine, Uva-Ursi, Buchu, Myrrh, Echinacea
Yemoja	Kelp, Squawvine, Cohosh, Dandelion, Yarrow, Aloe, Spirulina, Mints, Passionflower, Wild Yam Root
Ogun	Eucalyptus, Alfalfa, Hawthorn, Bloodroot, Parsley, Motherwort, Garlic
Oya	Mullein, Comfrey, Cherry Bark, Pleurisy Root, Elecampane, Horehound, Chickweed
Ṣango	Plantain, Saw Palmetto, Hibiscus, Fo-ti, Sarsaparilla, Nettles, Cayenne

The generally accepted way to prepare these herbs is as follows: The herbs are added alone or in combination to a kettle of mildly boiling water. Steep for approximately thirty minutes before straining. The remaining herbal solution is then prepared as a drink. In some instances, the herbal solutions are used in diluted form for enemas. Sugar should never be added to herbal solutions. Honey or lemon may be used sparingly.

Omiero: Spiritual Baths

Spiritual baths require the following:

A

1. That the correct herbs are used. The formula is based upon divination by the priests and priestesses. The presiding oriṣa or egun is determined and the corresponding herbs are obtained and prepared.

2. That the spiritual baths be continued for the number of days specified. The number can range from 1 to 21 days. This is also determined by divination or a reading.

3. During the period specified for the taking of spiritual baths there's to be light eating, sexual abstinence, emotional balance, and no use of intoxicants. Daily prayer and affirmations need to be said as well.

4. Before taking spiritual baths make sure that you set up your space. There are a number of things that you need to do in order to prepare yourself.

B

1. You need a white sheet or large towel to wrap yourself in and a white cloth to cover your head immediately after the bath.

2. Your space should be cleansed with incense.

3. The tub, sink, and vessel that will hold the spiritual bath should be clean. Other areas involved should also be clean.

4. White candles should be lit in the bathroom and any other areas involved.

5. Silence or meditative sounds should prevail.

6. Keep spiritual bath concentrates in the refrigerator when not in use, and always label the bottle!

C

The spiritual bath does not require that you sit in a tub. This is an immersion and should be specifically prescribed by the diviner or herbalist. The herbal solution should be diluted with water at a 12:1 or 8:1 ratio. (Example: 12 parts water to 1 part herbal solution.) The water should be cool or tepid, but never hot. Shake the herbal solution well before pouring it into the *igba je* (basin or large gourd). It really doesn't matter which goes in first, but it's easiest to measure the solution first, and then add the water.

1. First bathe or shower with natural soaps and shampoos.

2. Dry off (optional).

3. Kneel reverently or stand with conviction in the tub or shower area.

4. Gently pour the diluted herbal solution over your body. Pray aloud or silently for peace and protection.

5. Lightly dry yourself off, wrap up in the white sheet, and cover your hair with the cloth.

6. Clean the tub, vessel, or sink by wiping it out with a mild cleanser.

7. Retire for study, meditation, or just quiet time. Relax.

> *Note: Early morning or late night are the preferred times to take a spiritual bath. You may take a regular bath or shower after at least four hours have elapsed, if necessary. Sisters, if you're menstruating or pregnant, ask the diviner to check specifically to determine if it's okay for you to take a spiritual bath or shower during these times.*

Spiritual baths are basically made by placing the specific herbs into a pot of heated water (see Table 7 for specific herbs and their orisa correspondence). The herbs are then set to boil. After the herbs have boiled (releasing the ase), they're strained. The solution remaining constitutes the spiritual bath. Various substances such as *efun* (sacred earth) and oils are added to enhance the ase as needed. The bath constitution is known as *omiero*.

Prayers are said over the herbs as they're being prepared. Osain, the divinity/orisa of botany and herbology, is invoked so that the healing elements will be forthcoming. One incantation to Osain is *Ase omo Osain, ewe Aye*:" The power of Osain's children, the plants of the Earth."

Spiritual baths are suggested to devotees who need to be cleansed of negative influences impacting their aura or essence. The herbal properties are absorbed into the human dimensions and assist in the dissipation of negative influences. Spiritual baths may also be prescribed as preventives in these regards. Many forms of Yoruba initiations involve the bathing of the initiate in the ewe in order to enhance one's ase. Religious objects are also bathed in omiero as a part of the consecration of those objects.

Table 7. Ewe (herbs) for spiritual baths.

Orișa	English (Herbs)	Spanish (Hierbas or Plantas)
Obatala	Sweet Basil Tropical Almon Green Calalu Wild Tobacco Sage	Albahaca Almendra Bledo Blanco Salvia Salvia-de-Castilla Paraiso Suco Blanco Malva Aquinaldo Blanco
Elegba	Balmony Guava Tobacco Sugarcane	Amansa Guapo Guayaba Tabaco Cano Abre Camino Mejoran Almaceyo Espartillo Albahaca
Ogun	Eucalyptus Tobacco	Eucalypto Tabaco Siempre Viva Maravilla Romerillo
Oya	Royal Poinciana	Flamboyan Cucaracha Caimito Yucca
Yemoja	Oregano Plantain Spearmint Laurel	Marjorana Platano Yerba Buena Verbena Canutillo Cucaracha

Oṣun	Papaya	Lechosa
	Wild Lettuce	Rompersaraguey
	Bonset	Caisimon
	Cinnamon	Cassava
		Boton de Oro
		Abre Camino
		Sauco Blanco
Ṣango	Sacred Ficus	Alamo
	Spanish	Coaba
	Mahogany	Cedar
	Cedar	Ceiba
	African Teak	Platano
	Plantain	Rompersaraguey
	Bonset	Cano
	Sugarcane	Zarzaparilla
	Sarsaparilla	
	Camwood	

The Oriṣa Internal

The highest purpose of esotericism is that of the internalization of concepts, philosophies, and ritual/religious practices. Internalization is the process that brings the devout to stages of development based on inner growth and understanding. If no religious practice or doctrine were internalized, then change wouldn't be possible, especially from a spiritual or religious standpoint.

Theosophical questions as to where the oriṣas literally dwell arise when devotees begin to sense the unfolding of an oriṣa's divine attributes from within. The answers are relatively simple: Yes, the oriṣas dwell within the human existence. Eastern and Western traditions alike maintain that the holy ones—sacred entities, prophets, angels, avatars, etc., do have a focal point in the vast dimensions of the human mind and body. Yoga chakras, as internal wheels of energy existing in the physical/spiritual body, are examined in this light. To add, the Hindu divinities are said to also sit in the center of each chakra. Hence, the corresponding with the orisas, as internal divinities.

Through actual experience and research, it has been noted that within the chakras— regardless of cultural persuasion—there exist psycho-hormones, nerve plexuses, and culturally defined divinities. The chakras, the orisas, and the behavioral modes that are related to them are presented in Figures 2 through 9. Upon study, it becomes evident that the chakra modes, with their Hindu gods (again, culturally defined), correspond to the attributes of the orisas.[8] Chakras also exist in Buddhism and Taoism.

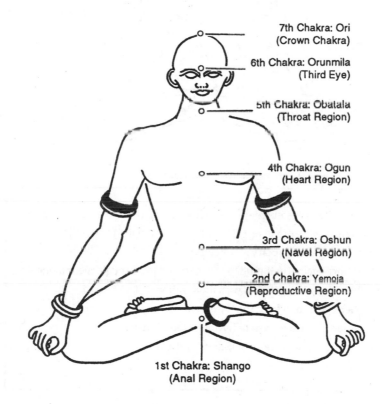

7th Chakra: Ori
(Crown Chakra)

6th Chakra: Orunmila
(Third Eye)

5th Chakra: Obatala
(Throat Region)

4th Chakra: Ogun
(Heart Region)

3rd Chakra: Oshun
(Navel Region)

2nd Chakra: Yemoja
(Reproductive Region)

1st Chakra: Shango
(Anal Region)

Figure 2. The chakras of the human body.

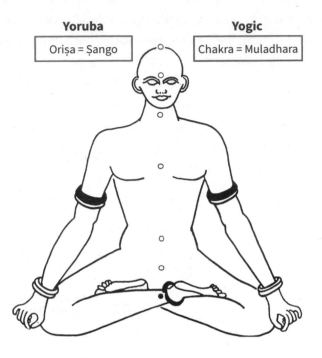

Yoruba	Yogic
Oriṣa = Ṣango	Chakra = Muladhara

Goals

1) Relax tensions in order to reduce karma and world entanglements.
2) Refine sense organs so that confusion and pain do not follow the seeking of temporary gratification.
3) Guard against polluting the sensory organs through overindulgence.
4) Begin to act wisely and with moderation.
5) Seek liberation from the lower realms.
6) Guard against violent behavior based on insecurity.
7) Be motivated towards self-development.

Figure 3. The first chakra.

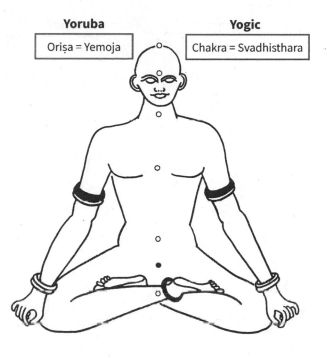

Yoruba	Yogic
Orişa = Yemoja	Chakra = Svadhisthara

Goals

1) Observe and study the effect of the moon upon the emotions.
2) Monetary wealth should precede fulfillment of sensual desires and sexual life.
3) Become free of base emotions such as anger, envy, and greed.
4) Remember always that a negative mind brings disaster.
5) Guard against being overly possessive.
6) Regulate primal needs in order to maintain your health.
7) Elevate the consciousness through fine arts and crafts.

Figure 4. The second chakra.

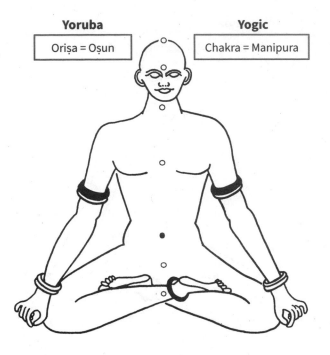

Yoruba

Oriṣa = Oṣun

Yogic

Chakra = Manipura

Goals

1) Recognize that using anger to control others leads to long-term failure.
2) Reflect more on the consequences of actions.
3) Guard against vanity and false pride.
4) Motivation is stimulated by the need for recognition, immortality, and power.
5) Seek to develop a positive ego and identity.
6) Give charity and selfless service.
7) Let love and compassion radiate from within.

Figure 5. The third chakra.

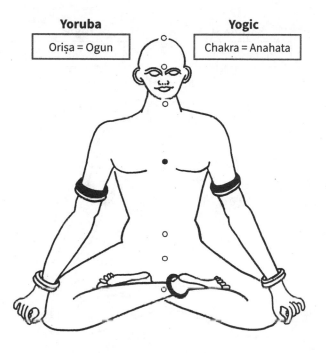

Yoruba

Orisa = Ogun

Yogic

Chakra = Anahata

Goals

1) Develop a higher sense of awareness and sensitivity.
2) Emphasize a sense of purity, innocence, and magnetism.
3) Reflect upon inner sounds (Nada Yoga).
4) Strive to become independent and self-emanating.
5) Strive to attain wisdom and inner strength.
6) Seek to control the breathing and heart rate.
7) Purity of relationships comes through the inner balancing of male and female energies.

Figure 6. The fourth chakra.

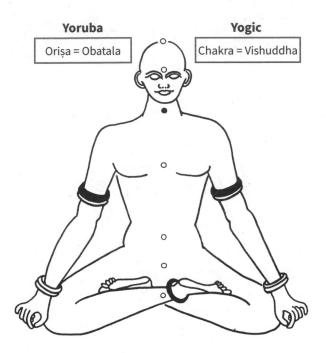

Yoruba

| Orişa = Obatala |

Yogic

| Chakra = Vishuddha |

Goals

1) Purify your sound to affect listeners in a positive way.
2) Awaken the dawning of awareness of eternal knowledge.
3) Supreme reason must overcome the emotions of the heart.
4) Use psychic energy and clairvoyance to communicate without words.
5) Guard against negative thought and use your knowledge wisely.
6) Become the master of the entire self.
7) Concentrate on the cooling mechanism (throat chakra).

Figure 7. The fifth chakra.

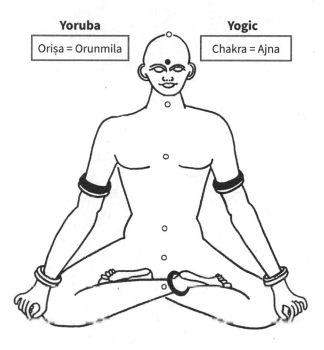

Yoruba

Orișa = Orunmila

Yogic

Chakra = Ajna

Goals
1) Meditate on the third eye to eradicate sins and impurities.
2) You reveal the divine within; you reflect divinity within others.
3) Practice austerity to bring about cosmic oneness.
4) Maintain proper balance through spiritual devotion.
5) Become One-Pointed. Become beyond the negative forces that pull one in many directions.
6) You may interpret the inner meanings of Cosmic Laws. You may generate scriptures.
7) You have the ability to induce visions of the past, present, future.

Figure 8. The sixth chakra.

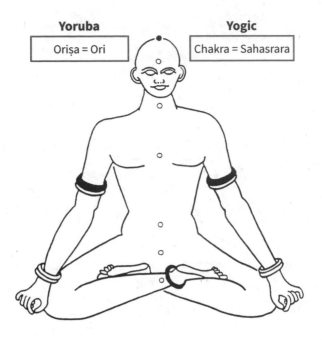

Yoruba

Orị̀sa = Ori

Yogic

Chakra = Sahasrara

Goals

1) Strive to reach the guru within. Through the consciousness one is able to attain oneness of all things.
2) Strive to lose the illusion of the individual self. Realize that the cosmic principles that govern the entire universe are within you also.
3) Strive to feel the divine and fully realize the divinity within.

Figure 9. The seventh chakra.

The following words in the Yoruba faith and practice lend to relative meditational insights:

1. Sise awo—training in metaphysical worship

2. Ikoso—self-control

3. Ifaiyabale—peaceful volition and nonviolence

4. Iwe mimo—spiritual teachings

5. Balaga—the state of consciousness when it first dawns

6. Isaro—meditation

7. Iwa-pele—deep sincerity and honesty of self; divine behavior

8. Idake roro—the discipline of silence

9. Imoye—knowledge

10. Da ma—quieting of the senses

11. Olumoye—guru/spiritual teacher

12. Eewo—undesirable behaviors that keep one in the flesh and earthbound

13. Ajaga—to yoke (as in the eight stages of yoga)

14. Apere—oneness with all things; liberation from earthbound desires

15. Aba—the act of directing the ase or universal energy

16. Toro—tranquility

As in other faiths, Yoruba devotees are not, as a whole, relegated to solely one way of life and practice. Adherents, devotees, and priests/priestesses are—and can/should be—involved in martial arts, yoga, tai chi, gymnastics, the armed forces, etc. As a result, the possibilities of comparative analysis become a natural occurrence. To say that Yoruba, as a civilization, only had priests and priestesses attending to oriṣas is off-centered. Clearly, there were merchants, soldiers, physicians, educators, musicians, engineers, farmers, tailors, and so on. And each individual had greater or lesser degrees of access to the metaphysical science of the time. Yet, regardless of their trade or profession the masses were involved in the faith and ritual of what we now call Ifa or Yoruba. Compare this view to any other civilization or culture; for example, not every Chinese person was a Shaolin Buddhist monk.

Prayer

"Prayer is the means by which the conviction that God is becomes instilled. God becomes, through prayer, a living force in the life of man. The real conviction that God is, comes to man not by belief that there is a God in the outer-world, but in the realization of the Divine within himself; and this realization is attained through prayer. . . . Prayer generates a moral force which not only changes our lives, but the lives of others also."[9]

In the Yoruba religion, *adura* (prayer) is very important. To make supplications to one's ori, the ancestors, oriṣas, Orunmila, and Olodumare is an essential part of Yoruba worship. It's to be understood that prayers to the divinities are for the purification and elevation of base human qualities. The highest form of prayer is that of the devotee asking for nothing except transcendence and protection from negating forces. By means of sincere prayer the devotee is better able to pass through the lower realms and attain the heavenly states.

Yoruba priests/priestesses are directed to assist devotees experiencing heavenly and earthly trials. Prayers to the deities for bearing children, finance, employment, marriage, and so forth fall under earthly tribulations. Prayers are strong voices against the oppressive earth forces that limit human stability and growth. By "calling on" the heavens the priestly are lending their voices to the eternal ether. Through the power of prayer, they seek to bring about change. The heavenly hosts are activated to combat or placate the detrimental forces.

Bringing about such changes for the sole purpose of worldly gains is considered sorcery. Prayer and sorcery—though similar in construct—are not synonymous. It's somewhat illogical to the divine psyche to place them together. When prayer is connected with the sacred unfoldment of the devotee, a sense of divinity arises. This divine rising is absent when sorcery is connected to a devotee's intent; clearly, the opposite or demonic is unleashed. Prayer ideally brings about divine intervention and the betterment of the devotee's person. Sorcery does not. If clearly examined, we can conclude that sorcery, again, brings about the opposite of transcendental development. Prayer, of course, enhances it. This is why the priestly are constantly directing the people in the way of the divine. The people mustn't fall victim to the forces of sorcery and illusion. It's as if to say "pray or be preyed upon"—in other words, pray or fall victim to disruptive forces.

It's important to set specific times and places for prayer. This disciplines the mind, which must be clear and focused in order to strengthen the endeavor. Dawn, or upon rising, is an especially good time for prayer as the mind and emotions have not yet been caught up in the world. At dawn, the ori is clear and the consciousness of the body is more open to creative sources of light and energy. Prayer before going to sleep is also potent. The aspirant then clears the ori of the daylong experiences and is set to rest from the worldly trials. The essence of spirit is reawakened and maintained throughout the dream-subconscious states.

For the Yoruba traditionalist, setting the proper atmosphere for prayer is duly important. Candles, incense, and bowls of water and fruits provide the spiritual essence that usually envelops a place of prayer or reverence. Musical instrumentation also plays a great part in setting the atmosphere. Yoruba devotees include drums, rattles, bells, handclaps, and song in the prayer directive. Prayers are often sung or chanted in rhythm and in harmony with the music. When prayers are said in the way of praise songs, they're called *oriki*. The oriki more specifically tell of the attributes and powers of the deities.

Devotees are set to learn prayers specific to their personal deities under the auspices of their priest. Novices aren't to over-extend themselves in the desire to learn all prayers. It's better to grasp what can be understood and go deep within. The prayers on the following pages to the orisa are a means to strengthen their religiosity through heavenly commune.

Although prayers are made at the shrines or altars of the given orisa, in no way is this a limitation. Prayers may be said at any time and in any place conducive to the elevating of one's self and one's spirit.

ORI

My Ori, it is you.
Ori, I hail you,
You who always remembers your devotee,
You who gives blessings to your devotee more quickly
    than other deities.

No deity blesses one without consent of their Ori.
A person whose sacrifice is accepted by their own Ori
Should rejoice exceedingly.

Ori, please do not shut the gate.
It is to you that I am coming.
Come and make my life prosperous.
It's Ori that brings fortune.

ẸṢỤ

Ẹṣu, protect my family.

Protect the initiates of the Temple and me also.

Let me not be moved against the people.

Let not the people be moved against me.

Grant me long life.

Grant me peace.

Grant me elevation of my consciousness.

Grant me the ability to use my own hands.

Ẹṣu, I salute you.

OBATALA

Orișa'ala, the great one who owns the world,
And to whom the control of the world must be assigned.
Obatala, Obatarisha, the orișa with authority
Who is as precious as pure honey.
The orișa with inexhaustible strength,
The inheritor of reputation
Whose great fame does not detract from his authority.
Obatala, save me!
One expects salvation from one's orișa.
I do not know how to save myself.

OṢUN

Oṣun, who is full of understanding.
Most gracious mother, Oṣun,
Most gracious oriṣa.
One who has large robust breasts,
One who appeases children
With brass ornaments.
Onikii who knows the secrets of cults,
But does not disclose them.
One who has a cool, fresh throne.
One who buries money in the sand.
The gracious mother, the Queen of the River Water
    which moves sleeplessly.
One who gives healing water free of charge.
One who gives good effective treatment to children.
One who has neither bone nor blood.
Ayila save me!
One expects salvation from one's deity.
I do not know how to save myself.
I give homage to Oṣun, Aṣẹ.

YEMOJA

Yemoja, mother of the fishes, Mother of the waters
 on the earth.

Nurture me, my mother.

Protect and guide me.

Like the waves of the ocean, wash away the trials
 that I bear.

Grant me children.

Grant me peace.

Let not the witches devour me. Let not evil people
 destroy me.

Yemoja, mother of all,

Nurture me my mother.

ṢANGO

Ṣango has come. Let every human being come and
    watch.
Ṣango, do not quarrel with me.
I am not one of them who is against you.
There are two solutions to a problem; Ṣango, please
    resolve them.
Obakoso, the powerful king,
My lord, the owner of the big royal drums,
Protect us from misfortune,
Protect us from illness,
Let us experience the calm and gentle things of life.

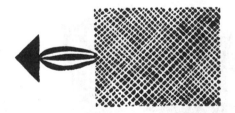

OGUN

Ogun, the powerful one,
Sufficiently great to stand before death.
One who makes human beings prosperous.
One who is not enriched by Ogun will
Find it difficult to get sacrificial kolanuts.
Ogun, enrich me.
Ogun, the powerful one,
The strong one of the earth,
The great one of the other world,
The protector of those who are being injured.
Ogun, support me.

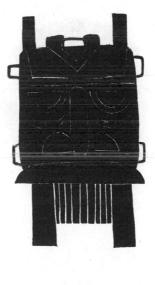

OYA

As powerful as the strong wind,

More fierce than the storm,

Oya, guard my soul against the many fingers of evil.

Help me to rest upon the earth free from strain and
undue frustration.

Oya, warrior of the wind, let not our land be overrun
with destroyers.

Let us not die in pain and sorrow.

Extend your weapon to protect us from destruction.

Oya, may we live and die to live again.

Oya, may our lives be long and our death short.

ORUNMILA

Orunmila, witness of fate second to Olodumare,
Thou art more efficacious than medicine.
Thou the immense orbit that averts the day of death.
My Lord Almighty to save Mysterious spirit that fought
    death—to thee salutation is first due in the morning.
Thou equilibrium that adjusts world forces, thou art the
    one whose exertion it is to reconstruct the creature of
    bad lot.
Repairer of misfortune—those who know thee become
    immortal.
My Lord, the un-deposable King, perfect in the house
    of wisdom, infinite in the house of knowledge; for
    not knowing thee in full, we are futile.
Oh, of we could but know thee in full, all would be well
    with us.

Ojubo: Sacred Places of Worship

The Yoruba refer to sacred places mainly as *ojubo* (the place of worship). If the place of worship is for an orișa, it's called *ile orișa* or *oju orișa*. If it's for the ancestors—an ancestral shrine or altar— then it's called *oju egun*. The major understanding that needs to be reached is, as Awolalu states, "The multiplicity of shrines stresses the fact that a shrine isn't a permanent or only abode of a divinity. . . . When the divinity is invoked, it is believed that the divinity will be present to meet with worshippers [regardless of the locale] to receive their prayers and offerings, and to bless them."[10]

Aborișa (devotees) generally present offerings as they pray to the orișas. *Ile* (temples, or "houses," as they're known in the New World) contain the shrines of a particular or group of orișa. Devotees attend the temples and are serviced by the priestly orders in the way of prayers, offerings, sacrifices, and ritual. Yet, as earlier stated, prayers and offerings need not be done solely at temple shrines; they may be done at the natural site of orișa essence. The earth or Onile itself is viewed as a shrine in this respect. Devotees may religiously seek the orișas from this perspective as well.

Yoruba forms of placing the body in positions of reverence are called *foribale*. *Moforibale* (I place my head to the earth) is the term that is solemnly uttered by devotees when homage is paid to the ancestors, orișas, or priests or priestesses. Males and females foribale differently, but this is not a gender statement. If the devotee has a female orișa as a "crown orișa," then foribale is done in a particular way. If the devotee has a male orișa as a "crown orișa," then another way of foribale is designated. It's the gender of one's orișa that determines the foribale, not that of the person.

Prostration or lying down in prone position with the forehead on the floor in front of the *ojubo* (shrine) or an *elegun* (person) mounted or possessed by an orișa most commonly done by those who have male orişa, while those who have female orişa place the right hip and elbow to the ground while putting the head on the right hand and then switching sides. All devotees prostrate themselves before queens, kings, chiefs, drummers, priests, those possessed, and babalawos. Or they kneel slightly, touching the right hand to the floor or ground. Added to this is *yikaa* (shoulder-to-shoulder greeting among the priests/priestesses)—three times: right, left, right—or among the iyawos—two times: right, left. Then there's *kunle* (kneeling in front of the shrine or elder person as a position of reverence, respect, and homage).

The emphasis of prayer is the opening of one's heart to sincerity of devotion and one's mind to the way of an *eniyan gidi* (authentic human being). The physical position taken is of secondary importance.

Ijuba: To Give Homage

The pouring of libation or *mojuba* (I give homage) is a prominent facet in regard to Yoruba reverence. The mojuba is given before all religious and social events. To give homage to the orişa, to the ancestors, to Olodumare, and to one's teachers or godparents is a necessary step that must be taken before any endeavor is begun.

Pouring libation is generally performed by those of the priestly or sacerdotal order. If there are none present, then an aborisa may pour libation. If that's not possible, then one who is spiritually motivated may do so. *Omi* (Water) is the element used in the pouring of libation. The priest/priestess pours small amounts on the floor, ground, or earth and recites the mojuba (see page 71). Infrequently, *oti* (gin) is used. Pouring libation is ritually done in front of shrines and at the onset of ceremonies, initiations, and cultural events, at the beginning of the day, etc. In the same way that other religions give homage to the core of their faith, so do the Yoruba. For example, the Hindu have *Surya Namaskar* (Sun Salutations) and Muslims pray or make *Salat* facing Mecca. In like manner, the Yoruba give prayer and homage to *Igigun Merin Aye* (The Four Corners of the Earth).

Igigun Merin Aye, mojuba re	To the Four Corners of the Earth, I give homage
Olojo Oni, mojuba re	To the Owner of the Day, I give homage
Mo n ji bara mo fon	I awake and present a clean body
Orisa gbogbo, ka n pe	All the orisa, we call (on you)
Alosun; 'Lorun; 'Labosun	The Spirit in the Daylight; The Spirit in the Sun; The Creator of the Deity who keeps the divining dust
Ta ji wa	That we awoke into the world and found it already here

At this point, the priestly offer incense or open palms to the four corners beginning with *ile-orun* (east), then *iwa-orun* (west), then *ariwa* (north), and finally, *guusu* (south). This is done while chanting *Olojo ni, iba se* ("To the Owner of the day, reverence is given").

Mojuba

Mojuba	I give homage
Omi Tutu	I present cool water
Ile Tutu	I present cool water to the temple
Ona Tutu	I present cool water to the road
Tutu Eṣu	I present cool water to Eṣu
Tutu Oriṣa	I present cool water to the oriṣas
Mojuba Olorun, Mojuba Olofi Mojuba Olodumare	I give homage to the various aspects of the Creator/God
Mojuba Ibae Egun Gbogbo Egun Ibae	I give homage to the ancestors
Mojuba Babal'oriṣa, Iyal'oriṣa Oluo Ara Orun	I give homage to the dead who bow at the feet of God
Mojuba Gbogbo Iku Nbelese Olodumare Iba'iye Orun	I give homage to the priestly and the elders of heaven
Ki Nkan Ma Se [state the names of godparents, mentors, guides]	Protect us, those of our spiritual lineage
Kosi Iku Kosi Arun Kosi Ofo Kosi Fitibo Kosi Idina Kosi Egba Kosi Ese Kosi Eyo	Help us to avert death, sickness, loss, stress, obstacles, paralysis, evil, tragedy
Ariku Babawa	Let us not see death, our Father
Ariku Iyawa	Let us not see death, our Mother

Ijo ati Orin: Dance and Song

Among the Yoruba, the expression of worship through dance and song is all encompassing. Every aspect of the religion finds its way through the human embodiment as movement and vocalization open the devotee to the aṣe of the ancestors or the orisa. Drewal writes, "through dance, spiritual forces materialize in the phenomenal world. The god is said to mount the devotee and, for a time, that devotee becomes the god. . . . Possession and trance states are often expressed through the medium of dance."[11] As in other devotional expressions, it's the priests/ priestesses who direct and monitor the dance and song of the orisa. They must be knowledgeable of the orisas as they manifest themselves through the human vehicle. Invoked through their particular dance patterns and song, the orisa "mounts" the priest or devotee. The priest must be able to invoke and channel the healing forces of the orisas in order to heal and also bring the people to *asuwada* (communal harmony and progression).

Dance, in respect to religion, is beyond the superficial taking of orisa dance classes. Orisa dance is a form of prayer and empowerment centered on the body temple. Orisa dance and drumming aren't separated from orisa worship in function, but the tones and rhythms and claves of the Yoruba can be found explicitly in African secular music throughout the world.

Novices of the religion are set to learn the sacred dances and songs. Much of these forms have come from the New World interpretations as expressed through Santeria and Lucumi. Frequent communal gatherings provide opportunities to dance and sing to the rhythm of bata drums or congas as a way of giving praise to orisas and invoking their power. The dance energy and movements reflect the natural attributes of the corresponding orisa. Obatala is slow and concentrated; Ogun is strong and rooted;

Yemoja is the tides of the ocean; Oṣun is graceful and expresses beauty; Ṣango is drawing lightning down from the sky; Oya is the whirlwind or hurricane; Elegba is balancing and flexible.

Some religious *orin* (songs) have been presented on the following pages so that devotees are better able to join in the communal giving of praise to the oriṣa. Numerous recordings and books on Yoruba have been produced.[12] Rhythmic patterns and melodies are more New World interpretation than Yoruba proper. Devotees may continually lend their own accent in order to feel elevated and at one with the heavenly states of being.

Elegba 1

Lead: Mojuba oriṣa, mojuba o, mojuba oriṣa
Chorus: Aṣe, mojuba oriṣa
        (Authority, I pay homage to the selected head.)

Lead: Mojuba o, mojuba oriṣa
        (I pay homage to the selected head.)
Chorus: Aṣe mojuba oriṣa

Lead: Mojubao mojuba oriṣa
Chorus: Aṣe, mojuba oriṣa

Lead: Iba oriṣa iba alaye o
        (Homage to the selected head, homage to the owner
        of the World.)
Chorus: Aṣe, mojuba oriṣa

Elegba 2

Lead: Iba'ra'go mojuba
               Iba'ra'go ago mojuba
               Omode koni'ko s'iba'go ago mojuba
               Elegba eṣu lona

Chorus: Repeat same.

(Homage to the relative of the Club. Give way, I pay homage. Child who teaches the doctrine of paying homage to the club, make way. I pay homage to the Owner of Vital Force [Aṣe], Eṣu is the one who owns the road.)

Lead: *Alagongon 'laro, agongon 'laroye* elegba de ma da nki o

Chorus: Repeat same.

(Owner of swiftness, owner of titles of honor. Swift-footed owner of titles. Owner of vital force come, but do not greet me only.)

Lead: Alagongon 'laro
Chorus: Laroye

Lead: Alagongon 'laro
Chorus: Elegba

Lead: Alagongon 'laro
Chorus: Eṣu l'ona

All: Alagongon 'laro

Elegba 3

Lead: Elegba o elegba nso yanga
               Alaroye mo da nkio
               Elegba nso yango

Chorus: Repeat same.

(Owner of vital force, owner of vital force, talking
pridefully. Owner of communication, I alone salute
you. Owner of vital force, talking pridefully.)

Obatala

All: Baba fu ruru, l'ore're o.

Oka yeye elejigbo

Eleri'fa, gba si gba sa wo.

Ejigbo re re gba si gba wo

E nu aye, eya wa l'oro

Eya wa l'oro elese'ka

(Father of the white cloth that rises and swells [like a
cloud].

Owner of the whips of profit.

Boa honored, honored Chief of Ejigbo

The Owner of the Head of Advantage strikes and
strikes [with a stick] just behold

Ejigbo's whips of profit, strike and strike behold

You clean the world.

Our tribe has the tradition

Our tribe has the tradition as supports of the boa.)

All: E nu aye mi mo so o

E nu aye mi baba

E nu aye mi mo se o

E nu aye mi baba

Obatala ta winiwini se ku're

Gbogbo la nya se rere

(You fill the world with life, knowledge accomplishes
it. You fill the world with life, father.

King of the White Cloth, a blessing,

All dream of warming the flow of goodness.)

Orunmila

Lead: Orunmila talade; baba moforibale
Chorus: Repeat same.

          (Orunmila owns the crown; father, I put my head on
          the ground.)

Egun

All: Egun mojuba iba e

          Egun mojuba iba e

          Egun gbogbo mojuba iba e

          Egun gbogbo mojuba iba e

          (I pay homage to the Ancestors. All pay homage to
          the Ancestors.)

Ogun

All: Ogun de are're ire gbogbo lo o ku aiye

          Ogun wa nile oke wa l'ona

          Ire gbogbo lo o ku aye

          (Ogun arrives, title-holder of Ire [township he
          founded].
          All of Ire proclaim, may you live forever in the world.
          Ogun comes to occupy the house.
          The mountain comes to have the road
          All of Ire proclaims, may you live forever in the
          world.)

Ori

All: Ori i mi, ori i mi, yo mi

          (My mind save [me].)

Oshoosi

All: Oshoosi o mo mi wara wara oke oke

Oba 'loke o mo mi wara wara oke oke

(Oshoosi you know me, quickly cherish [me] cherish [me]

King who owns the mountain, you know me quickly.

Cherish [me]

Cherish [me].)

Chorus: Repeat.

Lead: Oshoosi ayilooda. Malamala de

Chorus: Repeat.

(Oshoosi, revolver that turns away famine, the
dazzling one arrives.)

Lead: Yaa be ileke iworo ode mata. ago olona

Chorus: Repeat.

(Let us quickly petition the uppermost caretaker of the
hunter's tradition, do not shoot. Make way, owner of
the path.)

Lead: S'ire s'ire

Chorus: Ode mata ore ore

Lead: Wole wole

Chorus: Ode mata ore ore

Lead: Yi're yi're

Chorus: Ode mata ore ore

(Uncover goodness, uncover goodness,

Hunter do not shoot, friend, friend

Enter the house, Enter the house

Hunter do not shoot, friend, friend

Turn goodness, turn goodness [to me]

Hunter do not shoot, friend, friend.)

Oṣun

All: Iya mi ile odo

               Iya mi ile odo

               Gbogbo aṣe, o bi ni sala maa wo e

               Iya mi ile odo

               (My Mother's house is the river.

               My Mother's house is the river.

               All powerful. Women that flee for safety

               habitually visit her.)

               Iya mi ile oro; ìya mi ile oro

               Gbogbo aṣe, ise mi saraa maa wo e

               Iya mi ile oro

               (My Mother, House of tradition;

               My Mother, House of Tradition

               All powerful, my deeds of charity habitually consult

               you.

               My Mother, House of tradition.)

               Repeat.

All: Bi'mo Oṣun gba ile le

               O su o. aṣe wole wu're

               (You sprout abundantly yes. Power enter the house;

               swell goodness.)

               Repeat.

Yemoja

All: Yemoja ase'sun, ase'sun yemoja

Yemoja ase'sun, ase'sun yemoja

Yemoja olodo, olodo yemoja

Yemoja olodo, olodo yemoja

(Yemoja is the Gush of the Spring,

The Gush of the spring is Yemoja.

The Mother of the Children of Fishes is the Owner of
the Rivers.)

Ṣango

Lead: Mo fori bo rere o ṣango to'kan o ya de

Chorus: Repeat.

Lead: A wa'nile onile o ku o

A wa'nile onile o ya

Chorus: Repeat.

(I use my head to be covered with good,

Sango is worthy, he who's tears arrives.

Owner of the Earth long life to you.

We come to the owner of the earth,

the owner of the Earth who tears.)

Oya

Call & Response:

Oya o ya ile o

Oya mo ba l'oro'ke

(Tearer, you borrow the house

The Tearer, I found, has the highest tradition.)

Ancestral Reverence

It's the ancestors who have interpreted and revealed the words of the universal construct. They have actualized the aṣe in regard to psychological and cultural expression. They have uncovered the inherent divinity and spirituality of human existence. The ancestors provide the ethics and worldviews of the tradition. Adherents to the tradition abide by the ancestral wisdom in order to develop themselves and the culture. Ways of behavior to ensure a good life are primarily ancestral statements. It's a good life that leads to a good death—a death that leads beyond the gate and is life everlasting. The *Alaaṣe* provide examples of right living as handed down by Yoruba ancestors.

1. Ifarabale: Composure

2. Owo: Respect

3. Suuru: Patience

4. Eso: Caution

5. Imo: Knowledge

6. Ogbon: Wisdom

7. Oye: Understanding

The Development of Self-Yoruba Philosophy

The Thirteen Guidelines for Yoruba Self-Development have also been handed down by Yoruba ancestors to further enhance right living. They are as follows:

1. There Is to Be No Practice of Wickedness.

    "Those who sow the seeds of wickedness plant them
    upon the heads of their children."
    "Verily, ashes fly back into the face of he who throws them."

2. There Is to be No Stealing.

   "Even if Man does not see; Olodumare sees."

3. There Is to Be No Selfishness.

   "Those who are selfish will come to bear their loads alone."

4. There Is to Be No Covenant Breaking or Falsehood.

   "The covenant breakers will be carried away by the Earth."
   "The sacrifices of covenant breakers and liars are not
   accepted."
   "Do not lie against companions. Do not break a covenant
   with an associate. Such acts verily bring about our sleeping."

5. There Is to Be No Hypocrisy.

6. There Are to Be No Acts of Atrocity Committed Against One's
   Neighbors

7. There Is to Be No Dishonoring or Disrespecting of Elders.

   "The relationship of service between Elders and Youth is to
   be strengthened continuously."
   "The hand of the young does not reach the high shelf. That
   of the Elder does not fit into the small gourd."

8. There Is to Be Protection of the Women.

   "Women are the flowers of the garden; Men are the fence
   around them."

9. There Is to Be Truthfulness and Righteousness.

   "Those who are truthful and upright have the blessings of
   the divinities."

10. There Is to Be Kindness and Generosity.

   "Kindness begets Kindness."

11. There Is to Be Sensitivity in Respect to Person-to-Person Relationships.

12. There Is to Be Chastity in Respect to Vows of Mates.

   "Man, do not seduce another man's wife; Woman, do not seduce another woman's husband."

13. There Are to Be Hospitable Directives.[13]

It's stated by Oba Oseijeman Adefunmi I that "the egun/ancestors are the determiners of what is moral and truthful in respect to life. The oriṣa do not dictate morality, the ancestors do." The "good life" is established by being respectful to the elders/ancestors. Their wisdom and life directives need to be studied and adhered to. By following proverbial wisdom and insight, and listening to ancestral voices, Yoruba devotees are led to inner strengths and worldly balance. It mustn't be forgotten that the tenets of Ifa itself are ancestral understandings and interpretations. The very culture is built upon this.

   "The ancestors are people who have distinguished themselves on the moral plane. They are therefore accorded great respect and are held up as models for the living to emulate. They act as a spur to good conduct and the living in turn honor them by offering libations as well as naming their children after them."[14] "The ancestors aren't worshipped in the way West Africans worship God. They're not the final authority in all matters, nor are they given the same attributes as the Creator. They're, however, revered, honored, and respected, not as gods, but as spirits and predecessors . . . who are next to the Creator."[15]

The area of reincarnation is seen as an extension of the ancestral being. The Yoruba word *tunde* reflects this. Babatunde (father returns), Yetunde (mother returns) are examples of the recognition of the spiritual essence which, in part, brings itself back. The greater importance appears not to be so much on the plane of souls reliving on and on through karmic planes, but on the constant reliving of morals and values. Ironically, to the Yoruba, the returning or reincarnating of the ancestral soul is desired. One strives to live righteously so that they may return from heaven to earth. By returning to the earth, good ancestral souls strengthen the lives and the spirits of their surviving descendants.

The Yoruba maintain that the soul of a deceased person either journeys to *orun rere* (good heaven) or *orun apadi/orun buruku* (bad heaven). Souls taken before their time become ghosts upon the earth until Olorun comes and delivers them to Orun. The realization of an afterlife is as foremost in Yoruba religion as any other. It has already been noted that the living of a good life is brought about by revering and emulating the ancestors. This life on earth does determine what occurs beyond death.

The understanding held by Yoruba priests/priestesses is that human beings contain a number of souls. And upon death, these souls are released and are each placed in the heavens or the earth according to the person's life and deepness of wisdom. It has been said by the elders that "death to those who die knowing is not like death to those who die unknowing." Those who have lived a cruel and abusive life go to the place where their souls can never be restored. They can never again return to the living. People who commit suicide also fall into this category.

The structuring of the individual according to the Yoruba ancestors is totally intertwined with the structuring of the community or tribal nation. The tribe or band becomes the focal point of identification. It provides the individual with a center for her or his sense of belonging, education in the ways of the world, and methods for transcendence beyond the worlds.

Each stage of the life cycle is complete with ritual and religious ceremony as the core, and social developmental directives as the outer expression. For the individual to be considered as part of the tribal nation, they must be initiated into it even though they're physically born into it. Through initiation the candidate passes beyond the natural mode and gains access to the cultural mode— that is they're introduced to spiritual values. In the Yoruba culture those who are uninitiated do not have the full blessings of the ancestors nor the tribe nor the oriṣas. The term for these persons is *ologberi*. This does not mean that the uninitiated are unblessed or are cast aside. It's simply a statement of reciprocity: the more

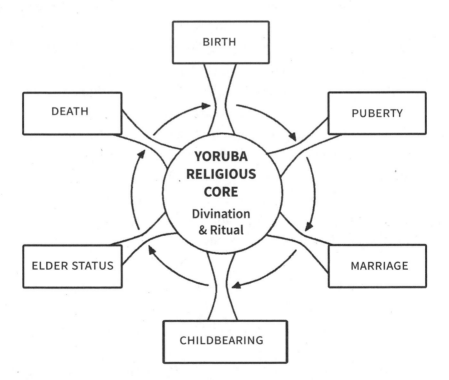

Figure 10. Traditional life stages of the Yoruba culture.

you involve yourself, the more you receive. This is a basic understanding in African religions, if not all.

Those who are initiated may grow to attain greater position and status within the family and the community. The *olori ebi* is the head of the extended family. She or he is responsible for rituals and judgments regarding the family. The *oba, baale, oloja* is the chief of the town or village. The *aworo* constitute the sacerdotal order. The *elegun* are the mediums. The *oloogun* are the medicine people/shamans. These positions provide a simplistic view of the multiplicity of strata that are a Yoruba community.

Yoruba social expression allows for polygamy, which is the marital condition whereby a man may have more than one wife. The key word here is *marital*. The man and the women involved are ritually embraced by both religious and social mores. They combine to form a productive unit geared toward interrelationship, childcare, business profit, and communal stability. The wives consider themselves sister-wives or co-wives with the emphasis on cooperation. The dynamics of polygamy are many, yet for centuries upon centuries Yoruba—as well as other world traditions—have continued to evolve both religiously and worldly under this form of social structure.

Yoruba religious expression also allows those of the priestly order to be married and raise children. Outside of specific sacred commitments, priests and priestesses are encouraged to marry. Orunmila, the prophet, was married to a number of wives and sired many children. The statement is clear that in respect to the ancestral way, male and female forces must be approached and balanced in order to create a stable person, and a stable family, community, and nation.

The creation of *egbe* (specific societies) is also an integral part of Yoruba communal functioning. The primary egbe follow:

Ogboni/Osugbo Society reflect the balancing of male and female forces in human construct and universal design. The Ogboni are headed by elders who revere the Earth Mother and strive to protect and uphold her purity. These elders are set to carry on the traditions of the ancestors. They also pass judgment on those who defy the traditional laws. Members are initiated into the society.

Egungun Society is devoted to the earth, but more so with the deceased who are buried in it. Those of the Egungun Society are mediums who have the ability to possess the spirit of those departed. They then communicate the desires and last messages to the family. The Egungun are known for their enormous masks and raffia dress with attached cloth covering their entire body.

Gelede Society is devoted to Yemoja. Their function is to bring about harmonious reconciliation between humans and the *aje* (witches). The Gelede cult wear masks with tribal markings and dress in padded clothing, representing the fullness of Yemoja. They invoke the witches and sacrifice to them in order to neutralize their powerful negativity and destructive potential.

· · ·4· · ·

DIVINATION, SACRIFICE, INITIATIONS

At the very center of the Yoruba religious practice and character development lay divination. As discussed in chapter 2, divination is perceived as that mystic state of communing with the divinities as revealed by Ōrunmila the Prophet. Every branch of Yoruba in the New World respects the various forms of divination born from the Ifa corpus. *Babalawo* (high priest), *baba'loriṣa* (priests), *iyal'oriṣa* (priestesses), and to some degree *aboriṣa* (Yoruba devotees) all use divination in order to:

1. Seek the scriptural messages of Ifa.

2. Inquire as to what offerings are expected by the oriṣa.

3. Inquire if the offerings are accepted by the oriṣa.

Divination implements differ at each level of the priesthood, yet all implements may be applied for revelations and inquiries to the divinities. The high priest uses the *ikin* (palm nuts) and *opon-Ifa* (divining board) and / or the *opele* (divining chain). The *o'loriṣa* (priests / priestesses) use the *merindilogun* (sixteen cowrie shells). The aborisa begin with the obi and *obi abata* (Nigerian kola nut) for the fundamental practice of divination. However, the obi and obi abata are also used by all levels of the priestly orders.

Obi Shell Patterns

The obi abata, the Nigerian kola nut, is split into four quarters, showing two male (*ako meji*) and two female (*abo meji*) sides. Yoruba diviners notate and interpret the quarters based on how they fall when cast. In the New World obi abata have been replaced by four pieces of a coconut shell with a cowrie attached to each piece.[1] Two males (shells that show the bulb side) and two females (shells that show the ridges) are cast. Divination is then completed in the same manner as the Nigerian Old World (as seen in Table 8).

The more general use of the obi abata is to ask yes or no questions of the orisa, the ancestors, or the ori of the seeker. The obi are also used to determine if an offering is acceptable to the orisa. The obi are cast and may land either faceup/concave ◯ or facedown/convex ⬤.

Prior to actually casting the obi, water is sprinkled on them by the devotee. The devotee prays to the obi, saying:

Ago obi, ago obi, ago obi
(Listen obi)
Obi ni ibi iku
(The obi averts death)
Obi ni ibi arun
(The obi averts sickness)
Obi ni ibi ofo
(The obi averts loss)
Obi ni ibi fitibo
(The obi averts being overwhelmed)
Obi ni ibi idina
(The obi averts obstacles)

In reference to the orisa approached either at the *ojubo* (shrine) or in the natural environment or sacred place, a prayer is also made. The devotee holds the obi in the left hand and with the right hand she/he knocks upon the floor or ground three times and incants:

Ile mo ki e o, Ile mo ki e o, Ile mo ki e o.
(Shrine I greet you.)

The obi are then placed in the right hand, and with the left hand knocking the devotee incants:

Ile mo ki e o iki eye. Ile mo ki e o iki eye. Ile mo ki e o iki eye.
(Shrine I greet you with honor.)

The obi are returned back to the left hand, and with the right hand knocking the devotee incants:

Obi [the name of orisa or egun] Ile mo ki e o iki eye.
(Obi [the name of orisa or egun] I greet you with honor.)
[Repeat three times.]

The various patterns that the obi can fall when cast and how to interpret them are indicated in Table 8.

Table 8. The patterns of an obi cast.

Obi	Pattern	Meaning
Alafia	○ ○ ○ ○	Yes
Etawa*	○ ○ ○ ●	Perhaps
Ejife	○ ○ ● ●	Definitely
Okana	○ ● ● ●	No
Oyeku	● ● ● ●	No

Note: When Etawa appears, cast again then make the determination based thereon. If Etawa appears on the second cast also, the answer is yes; Etawa implies struggle, or not giving oneself enough aṣe.

Figure 11. Here is an example of a traditional opon Ifa *(divining board) using palm nuts. The obi cast shows* Ejife *(see Table 8), meaning "definitely" to a question asked to the orisa. The only consideration here is whether the shells face up or down. Male and female cowries are not taken into account.*

If the obi fall in patterns indicating a yes response, then not much more needs to be done. If the fall indicates a no response, then the priestly or devotee must continue to state other offerings. After each statement the shells are cast again. This process is repeated until a yes pattern appears. In this manner, it's determined if offerings have been accepted or if the intent or desire of the devotee is acceptable to the orişa or egun.

Ifa Revelations

Divination that focuses more on the revelations of Ifa is divided into four dimensions. These dimensions are studied by the initiates on a continual basis. The dimensions of divination are integral parts of each other. They may be developed and expounded upon separately, yet in actual practice they overlap and blend into a oneness which is the foundation of divination. The four dimensions are supported by four steps:

1. Divination: The casting of obi, merindilogun, opele, or ikin.

2. Notation: In writing, speech, or mind, the recording of the number and/or patterns. In Yoruba proper—the Odu.

3. Interpretation: The use of proverbs, stories, experiences, etc., that are based upon the Odu cast and noted. As such, the diviner gives the seeker the nature of his or her concerns as well as supporting psychological and spiritual insights and directives.

4. Application: Based upon all of the above, this is what the seeker is to do. This may be as involved as complex cleansing rituals or as simple as wearing a particular color. Application, in a sense, has at heart the offering of one's self-energies to the orişa and/or egun for the elevation, the spirit, and the aversion of the dangers in one's life.

Before the obi abata are cast, mojuba is offered (see page 69). The devotee now places the shells or the actual split kola nuts into her/his hands. Upon gently shaking them, the devotee chants:

Akinmoran, Akinmoran, Akinmoran

May the divine spirit in heaven assist the divine spirit on earth.

The devotee then exhales on the shells three times and places them (still cupped in her/his hands) to the forehead. Now, with the words *dida obi* (cast obi for), the name of seeker is said and the shells are released on the *kekere opon* (little divining tray) or *ate* (mat or white cloth). The character is determined, and the counseling begins. To determine the character is the first degree of interpretation. See Table 9.

Table 9. Obi abata interpretations.

Characters	Obi Abata	Directive
Ilera	1 Male shell	Health, Status
Aje	1 Female shell	Finance, Material and Money
Ejire	1 Male and 1 Female shell	Friendships, Relationships
Ero	2 Female shells	Love, Marriage
Akoran	2 Male shells	Stability, Peaceful Development, Upliftment
Akita	2 Male and 1 Female	Success after Hardship, Controversy
Obita	2 Female and 1 Male	Home Situation and Environment
Ogbe	All shells up	Justice, Righteousness
Oyeku	No shells up	Transformation, Rebirth

Note: The direction in which the shell(s) point is also of great importance.

The direction of the shells is the next degree of interpreting that the novice must study. If the shell closest to the top is male and points to the right or top, then the interpretation of the situation is positive. If the male shell points to the left or toward the bottom, then a negative interpretation is made. If the shell closest to the top is female and points to the right or bottom, then a positive interpretation is made. If the female shell points to the left or toward the top, then a negative interpretation is made. In either case the healing messages of the diviner must lend to the elevation of those seeking assistance.

The third degree of interpreting the obi abata is to determine the Odu by the concave and convex fall of the shells from the top of the opon to the bottom. The concave is open and marked as I (light). The convex is closed and marked as II (dark). (See Figure 1 on page 15 for the sixteen major Odu.) The patterns are those of the opele as examined in chapter 2 (Ifa Corpus), and the Odu may be examined as done by a babalawo. Only the initiated need work to this degree as sacrifices are necessary.

The *merindilogun* (sixteen cowries) represent the third level of Ifa divination. They're only to be used by the priests and priestesses of the orisa order. The sixteen cowries are part of the consecrated religious objects obtained when an aborisa is initiated into the orisa sacerdotal order. They should not be used by the uninitiated.

Once this level of Ifa divination is attained, the ase of the Odu, the orisa, and all the spiritual forces of the Yoruba planes of realization become actual. The process of learning and fortifying the initiate is the responsibility of the godparent, priest, mentor, and so on. Nowhere in Yorubaland are the Odu approached lightly. And as the merindilogun reflect the Odu, nowhere are they taken lightly. The reasons for providing the divine expressions of the shells are to accomplish the following:

1. Elevate the respect level for them as to what they represent.

2. Erase the ignorance of so many devotees who are literally being taken advantage of due to their lack of knowledge.

3. Stimulate interest in devotees so that they further investigate Yoruba sacerdotal orders intelligently and spiritually.

◊ ◊ ◊

The forces of *orun* (heaven) and *aye* (earth) are unfolded through the Odu. The diviner must prepare for the immersion into Ifa realms. The mojuba is given; prayers are said (particularly to the orisa of the shells being used). The shells are rubbed between the diviner's hands as prayers for the seeker are offered. The shells are then placed in a sacred bowl and presented to the seeker who exhales on them three times. The diviner then touches the forehead of the seeker with the shells (enclosed in his/her hands) and the cast is made with the words, *difa fun* (cast Ifa for) the name of the seeker. Then a second cast is made so that a double Odu results. The first is dominant, the second is the balancing factor. How the shells fall in respect to the female sides showing, or shells up, determines the Odu. Table 10 presents the merindilogun. The order of the Odu is different for the o'lorisa than for the babalawo as cited on page 12. Although they're interpreted basically the same, the babalawo has deeper insights and revelations.

Table 10. The merindilogun cast and their order.*

Okanran	1 shell up
Oyeku	2 shells up
Ogunda	3 shells up
Irosun	4 shells up

Ọṣe	5 shells up
Obara	6 shells up
Edi	7 shells up
Ogbe	8 shells up
Osa	9 shells up
Ofun	10 shells up
Oworin	11 shells up
Oturupon	12 shells up
Ika	13 shells up
Iwori	14 shells up
Otura	15 shells up
Irete	16 shells up
Opira	No shells up

*The merindilogun are cast twice. If the same Odu appears on the second cast the term *meji* is added. For example, Okanran cast twice is Okanran Meji. If the second cast is different than the first, then the Odu is called accordingly. For example, if the first cast is Okanran, and the second Otura, the cast is called Okanran-Otura.

The Ikin and the Opele

The ikin and the opele are the fourth-level reflections of the divine Odu. This is the level of the Odu as interpreted by the high priest of the Yoruba tradition. The high priest is known as an Ifa priest or *babalawo* (father of mysteries). Only he or she (*iyalawo*) is permitted to use the *ikin* (sacred palm nuts), and the *opele* (divining chain) for the purpose of divination. The ikin are deemed sacred because of Orunmila. He ordained that they would be the symbols of his divine being and presence on earth. The ikin, as with the later developed opele, are presented to the babalawo or iyalawo apprentice after initiation.

Divination on this level yields the greatest insight into the cosmic intelligence and spirit-energy of the Odu. This insight yields the deepest of understandings and interpretation of the Odu and the divinities who exist within them. By "pounding" the ikin or casting the opele, the diviner is able to determine the Odu which, in the mystic sense, calls down the heavenly entities. The babalawo/iyalawo must be able to recall and recite messages pertinent to the seeker's situation. He/she must also be able to devise and develop workable and applicable ways for the seeker to be elevated through or by means of *ebo* (sacrifice). For these reasons the babalawo is the final mortal messenger. Priests and priestesses of the orisa consult the babalawo in times of difficulties and to attain greater insight into the religion. Members of the Yoruba tradition view the babalawo as the epitome of cultural maintainers and the guides to inner awareness, spiritual elevation, and soul salvation.

Before the cast is made, the babalawo prepares himself through prayers to Orunmila, chants, and contemplation. Prayers for the seeker follow. The babalawo then takes the divining implements and presents them to the seeker. The seeker exhales upon the ikin or opele three times. The exhalation is done so that the *emi* (inner spirit) may activate the divining apparatus to focus on the seeker specifically.

Ebo: Offerings and Sacrifices

It has been stated throughout the previous chapters that offerings and sacrifices are presented to the orisas (and to the egun). In Yoruba, ebo is divided into two categories. But before addressing this controversial issue, let me begin by saying that I am neither a proponent or opponent of blood sacrifices. It has, however, been part of human history across many cultures. In my practice of Yoruba I have, however, replaced its ritual practice with more concentrated work both within myself and within my community.

With this in mind, let's examine the two types of offerings.

- *Ebo*: The offering of any plant or object that has been first used to spiritually cleanse oneself (baths, rubbing fruit over the body) and offerings that involve the work of the devotee, such as cooking food and carving statues.

- *Adimu*: The offering of clothes, plants, and fruits; cooked or uncooked foods; and tangible objects to the orişas not prepared or carved by the devotee.

Divination by one's priest or priestess determines the type of ebo and/or adimu that's prescribed. Yoruba practitioners rarely go about invoking the deities or presenting sacrificial offerings to them without first consulting the diviners. Ebo is prescribed, in one form or another, whenever Ifa is consulted. This is because of the Yoruba belief in the "reciprocity of aşe." The heavenly forces are reverently invoked and prayed to and are expected to respond to the devout, granting their supplications and providing protection from malevolent forces. In return, the devout are expected to replenish the aşe through sacrifice and offerings. Many times, greater devotion and the sincere effort to change our wayward behavior is also expected—if not primarily.

Human cultures have always practiced multiple forms of sacrifice for religious purposes. Although the forms may be questioned, the purpose remains the same: the human attempts to reach the divinity through themselves and their world. What continues to be misunderstood is that sacrifice—in the physical or spiritual sense—is an active proponent of all religious involvement.

The most ancient builders of nations, such as the Khemetians of Africa, the peoples of India and China, and other Asian countries all have religious accounts of blood sacrifice and prescribed offerings to the deities of their culture. Near Eastern countries, such as Israel, Jordan, and others, have lent biblical testaments which give credence to blood sacrifice—especially for the atonement of sins. Native Americans sacrificed to their cultural deities, as studies of the Aztecs so clearly reveal. Tribal nations across the North and South American continent sacrificed to earth and sky deities. Europeans also practiced the way of sacrifice. For example, in Homer's *Odyssey* it's said that Odysseus made sacrifice of sheep for the dead. The ancient Greeks, Romans, and tribal nations of European origin made continual offerings and sacrifices to their gods.[2]

Reasons why offerings are given:

- To give thanks for the granting of a need or desire.

- As a promise or sacred vow made to the deity.

- To prevent the cause of suffering.

- To remove the cause of suffering.

- As a way of substituting the sacrificial animal for the devotee.

- To provide strength, stability, and courage to achieve in the visible world, as well as the invisible world.

The sacred act of sacrifice, or "making ebo," is comprised of four parts:

1. The priest presents the devotee and the ebo to the holy symbol representing the deity.

2. Prayers over the devotee and to the ebo are made to consecrate them.

3. The deity is invoked to participate and receive the offering.

4. The offering is placed at the shrine of the deity as prayers are said.

Offerings, however, are only one aspect in the complexity of ritual. Prayer, dance, symbolic gestures, and personal and communal elevation are all active elements in sacrificial ritual. These elements are combined to "call down" the oriṣa in Yoruba practice. Novices mustn't be led into believing that "making ebo" is the highest form of sacrifice that will make everything right in a world gone wrong. To make ebo is to open the opportunity for positive change and to enhance the possibility of growth. The human factor mustn't be overlooked. The greatest sacrifice is the human sacrifice—the sacrificing of negative thoughts and destructive tendencies; the sacrifice of the lower-based self for the divine principle of being. All other sacrifices are intended to enhance this human endeavor.

Types of offerings presented to the egun and/or oriṣa are:

- Spiritual baths
- Medicinal herbs
- Prayers and meditation
- Offerings of fruit, flowers, tobacco, cloth, or foods of the oriṣa
- Socially charitable acts
- Fruit and flower cleansings
- Incense and oils
- Self-reflective directives
- Altars and shrines
- Stronger religious involvement

- Song and dance
- Flaws of character

Table 11 gives examples of the various foods and animals offerings that may be offered to the specific oriṣa. Remember, offerings are done under the guidance of qualified priests/priestesses. It's strongly advised that no invocation or offering be made without their knowledge or approval. See Tables 11 and 12 for information about offerings and objects associated with the oriṣa.

Table 11. Offerings to the oriṣas.

Oriṣa	Sacrificial Offerings
Obatala	White fruits, coconut, white kola nuts, efun (sacred earth), white yams, snails, snail water, shea butter, rice, hens, pigeons, female goats
Elegba	Palm oil, tobacco, all fruits/nuts, roasted corn, coconut, roosters, male goats, yams
Oṣun	Honey, cinnamon, pumpkin, lettuce, oranges, eggs, guinea hens, hens, sheep
Yemoja	Molasses, cooked seafoods, ducks, hens (or roosters), objects from the ocean
Ogun	Palm wine, rum, palm oil, pineapple/fruits, roasted corn, tobacco, roosters, male goats, yams
Oya	Rum, red wine, eggplant, rice and beans, plums, tobacco, purple grapes, hens (or roosters), female goats, plantains
Ṣango	Plantains, yams, okra, green bananas, tobacco, rum, bitter kola nuts, rams, roosters (red), branches of trees struck by lightning, etc.

Table 12. Objects associated with each oriṣa.

Oriṣa	Objects Associated with Each Oriṣa
Obatala	Elephants, white birds, statues of elder African men dressed in white, images of mountains, white cloth
Elegba	Statues of male figures and/or long-braided hair, rocks, coconuts
Oṣun	Fertility artifacts, objects of brass or gold, peacock feathers, mirrors, fans, fine jewelry, cowrie shells
Yemoja	Strong matriarchal statues, creatures of the sea, shells from the sea, images of the sea
Ogun	Machetes, all iron objects, statues of hunters and warriors, blacksmiths, vehicles of iron or metal
Oya	Buffalo horns, grotesque masks, multicolored cloth, images of storms
Ṣango	Double ax (oṣe Ṣango), black cats, ram heads, drums, stones, trees struck by lightning, horses, turtles

Initiation into the Priestly Realms

Being a priest or priestess involves the merging of one's personality into a much larger whole. Humility, subjugation to oriṣa and to the discipline of ritual are essential qualities for a priest/priestess to achieve. So, for the oriṣa priest/priestess, modesty and a complete lack of selfishness are the prerequisites of wisdom.

—Yoruba Priestly Wisdom of Baba Ifa Karade

The process of becoming a Yoruba priest or priestess is defined by marked stages of ritual ceremony along with related teachings. Novices embarking on this journey must first find a *babalawo* or *iyalawo* (high priest/priestess, respectively) or an *o'loriṣa* (priest/priestess) who will provide them with the nurturing and patience so strongly needed. There should be relatively little conflict or "bad vibrations" between *aboriṣas* (novices) and the priests. The two must work harmoniously to achieve the goal or objective, which is to guide the novice to a point of insight, understanding, and capability on the one hand and to increase the insights and skills of the priestly initiators on the other.

Not all people who involve themselves in oriṣa practice need to become initiated into the priestly sacerdotal order. Many find solace in achieving any one of the various stages available to them. Yoruba provides, in New World practice, a number of levels of achievement. The following reflects five of these levels. They're by no means the only stages, but they're the foremost ones.

Receiving the Ilekes: Sacred Beads

Ilekes are the religious beads that mark the first level of actual commitment made by the novice. Five ilekes are presented ceremoniously to the initiate. Each ileke represents an oriṣa:

white—Obatala; black and red—Elegba; yellow—Oṣun; blue—Yemoja; red and white—Ṣango. The ilekes are consecrated by the presiding priest or priestess. *Ewe* (herbs), *ebo* (offerings), and *efun* (sacred earth) are made into a solution called *omiero*. The ilekes are washed in the solution and are now consecrated. They now have the aṣe, which will empower the devotee with the essence of the oriṣa.

Receiving the Ajagun: Warriors

The word *ajagun* is Yoruba for warriors. The ajagun are comprised of Elegba, Ogun, Oshoosi, and Oṣun. Their function is to protect the aborisa from destruction by oppositional spiritual forces (*ajogun*) and oppositional people (*omo-aiye*). In no way should this be interpreted as sorcery or witchcraft. All religious systems provide their believers with protectors against the demonic. Yoruba is no different.

Those temples that express love and light infuse that energy into the aṣe of the consecrated ajogun. In doing so, protection is a worthy response of the angelic *irunmole* (entities of light and transcendence). Hence, there's little to fear from "negative forces." Those temples that express conflict and confusion lend this energy to the aṣe of the ajogun and hence the perpetuation of that energy.

Onifa: The One Iland of Orunmila

This ceremonial ritual involves the initiate more so with the aṣe of Orunmila and the Odu. Devotees receive the consecrated objects of Orunmila: the *ikin* (sacred palm nuts), the *agere* (the container for the ikin), a yellow and green *ileke* (necklace / collar), and the *ide* (religious beads formed as a wristlet). The ide is worn on the left wrist and is Orunmila's symbol to *iku* (death) that the devotee is a "child of the prophet" and shouldn't be taken before their time. The babalawo uses his ikin to determine the Odu, which are the heavenly disciples present to guide the initiate to sacredness and divine wisdom. The initiate is instructed on how to pray using the ikin and how to call upon her/his Odu for worldly assistance and spiritual elevation. Only the babalawo/iyalawo can preside over this ritual.

Elehan or Isese or Ocha: Priesthood

At this stage, the initiate is proclaimed ready to serve as priest or priestess. They have demonstrated their degree of commitment and have stood the test set upon them by oriṣa, ancestors, and godparents alike. There are different reasons why one is called into the priesthood. Some are called for spiritual reasons that involve only themselves and they work very little with others; some are called to be *ojise* (messengers of the faith). Others are called to serve the oriṣa in order to uplift humankind from the muck and mire of the mundane.

Elehan/Isese/Ocha may last from three to seven days. During this time the initiate/*iyawo* (bride of the oriṣa) is set to undergo a series of trials and teachings so that the priestly abilities and understandings are crystallized. She or he must reside in the *ile* (temple) during the entire time. Fasting, abstinence, internal study, learning about the oriṣa, divination, and daily offerings are all focused on during this period. Drumming, sacred dance, and communal worship are also parts of the initiation. The temple is full of images that reflect the oriṣa that will "own the head" of the new o'loriṣa. On or about the third day, divination is performed. This is the day of the Ita. The Ita reveals—through the Odu—the messages to be seriously contemplated and acted upon by the new priests/priestesses for the entire time of their priestly involvement and endeavors. The period of apprenticeship lasts from three months to one year depending on the will of the oriṣa, as determined through divination.

Only those who have made elehan can preside over those making elehan. The presiding priest/priestess is responsible for the development of the initiate through the period of the initiation or, to a greater degree, when the iyawos are able to establish and maintain their own temple and *aborişa* (godchildren). Another priest/priestess is deemed the *ajubona* or instructor. The ajubona has the responsibility of teaching the iyawo the constructs of the Yoruba religion and of breaking down the revelations of the god-parent to more applicable workings.

On the final day of initiation, the iyawo receives the Odu-orişa, which is a wooden or clay container holding the aşe of the specific orişa. Inside are the religious objects consecrated to the orişa. The objects have been consecrated by means of herbal washings, offerings, cleansed by incense, song, and prayer. The New World directive is to present the "crown orişa" along with four others of the set. For example, if the aborisa making elehan is to be a priestess of Oşun, she would also receive Elegba, Obat-ala, Şango, and Yemoja. The elder Yoruba directive is to present only that orişa who is the "crown orişa" of the initiate. No other orişa are received during this time unless so determined through divination.

The function of the initiation rituals is to make the orişa essence stronger within the devotee. The more rituals that are done, the more this essence is solidified and actualized. The essence then impacts upon the being of the devotee who now becomes an active element of it within the family, community, nation, and world. Those who pass through the various levels must intensify their lives through constant prayer, devotion, and sacrifice to the orişa. Those who become priests/priestesses must understand their position as seen through the eyes of heaven more so than the eyes of earth. They have the sacred duty to assert and reassert the divinity of all human beings. That is, they work to elevate the base human nature to divine nature.

Babalawo: High Priest

Those who become babalawo are the high priests in the Yoruba culture. They're often revered for their humility, conviction, faith, honesty, and sincerity. Basic and stringent codes of conduct were laid down by Orunmila to the elder Ifa priests to ensure that this order not be corrupted in its ideals. Those priests who do not abide by the code will be punished by Orunmila.

Professor W. Abimbola writes and lectures on the subject of the babalawo. He states, "the training of an Ifa priest is a supreme example of sacrifice in human endeavor. . . . The aim of the training is to give the priest-in-training a disciplined attitude to the many problems in life. . . . It was therefore the primary aim of the training to prepare him adequately to meet the grave responsibilities of important positions in the community."[3]

The initiation into Ifa is primarily done for and by male members of the culture. Women have also explored the intense energies of the Odu-Ifa. The ordained men and women must follow strict rules for admittance. Those infants who are divined to become a babalawo begin the actual ritualization at age seven. Older members of the culture may also become initiated if revealed through Ifa.

Itefa

The ritualization process for babalawo initiation is called Itefa. The process lasts from three to fourteen days and is presided over by a babalawo. The aspirant is shaved of all facial hairs and led to the *igbodu* (sacred hut) built for the ritual. Inside the igbodu the babalawo initiate undergoes the secret trials. Upon its completion, the *kekere awo* (little bit babalawo) emerges. He is now ready to do the following:

- Study the Ifa corpus

- Learn the way of the divination implements

- Become proficient in the way of offerings and ritual

- Become the epitome of divine nature among the people

Etutu: Rituals

Rituals make us no longer passive beings in the cosmos, but we become creative agents of existence.[4]

Rituals generate a sense of certainty and familiarity. They provide continuity among those who perform or attend them. In turn people find a degree of identity through its common observance and experience.[5]

It's important to designate the space and time that rituals are to be performed. To the Yoruba, order is of the utmost importance. The ability to effectively conduct a ritual ceremony is the responsibility of the presiding priest or priestess. They must ensure that all stages are complete and that transitions from one level to the next are smooth. Supporting temple members ensure that the directives of the presiding o'lorişa or babalawo are carried out effectively.

The ritual is harmonious and creative. There is no need for ill energy to exist, as this opens the way for negating beings to disrupt the sacred objective. Rituals need not be sterile or done by rote. To create is to recreate the infinite magnitude of nature's expression. The important statement is that the presiding o'lorişa must be sensitive to the spirit of the initiate and set the initiation or ritual accordingly.

There are rules and guidelines that need to be adhered to by priests/priestesses and devotees alike:

1. There's to be a period of sexual abstinence (at least 24 hours) before and after the initiation.

2. No over-the-counter/prescription drugs are to be taken (unless absolutely necessary for health purposes) on the day of the ritual.

3. There's to be no use of intoxicants or drugs.

4. Novices must bathe and take spiritual baths before the ritual begins.

5. Novices must be well aware of the purpose for the ritual.

6. After the ritual, initiates must rest for at least one day.

◊ ◊ ◊

As novices begin to contemplate Yoruba as a religion and/or cultural expression, it's important to understand ritualization. All too often the misconception is that academic research and passive involvement are sufficient, that following a course is better than flowing with the essence of worship internalized. The result is the production of a less than open mind and spirit. Rituals performed must serve to open the devotee and make them more receptive to the aṣe of the teachers, ancestors, and oriṣa. The ritual is seen as spiritual and is done to bring about the cleansing and heightening of the spirit. In other words, spiritual enlightenment and elevation are the ends to the means of rituals—specifically religious ones.

Social rituals performed at marriage, childbirth, and death appear to be nonreligious. However, social rituals have, as the core, religious substance. It's priests or priestesses who perform the weddings, lead the Stepping Into the World for infants, and preside over funerals. Yes, these stages of life may be done without ritual, but the way of societies is to build our life cycles within and through rituals and vice versa. There appears to be something basically human—or even total in the life cycles of animals—about rituals from birth to mating to childbearing and to death.

The spirit is not considered the soul of a person, although the words are often used interchangeably. It's the spirit, once enlightened and elevated, that frees the soul. The spirit is the bonding essence of human nature with divine nature. The soul is the inner flame that exists as a cinder or spark arising from the creative fire.

CONCLUSION

The Yoruba religion is a viable and time-honored way of life. Those who seek to change their relationship with themselves, the world, and universal forces may consider Yoruba a possible vehicle. Seekers of the inner self may embrace Yoruba as a source of light and as a source of esoteric teachings. It's important to continually review the contents of this book. Degrees of acceptance and resistance to areas of specific study need to be weighed and discussed openly and maturely.

The true objective of Yoruba religious involvement is to live according to ancestral wisdom and divine righteousness. By embracing the Odu of the Yoruba philosophy, you embrace the purity and religiosity of the tradition. By accepting the rituals, initiations, and teachings as your own, you may sense the dawning of spirit and the emergence of your soul. Follow the true objective.

As you study the Yoruba religion, keep in mind that intellect and academia alone aren't enough. The student or devotee of Yoruba must also be immersed in ritual, because it's through rituals and initiations that the essence beyond the intellect is awakened. That essence is spirit. The culture of the religion must be accepted, for culture and religion cannot be separated. When you have finished reading, you will need a spiritual guide—a mentor. Yoruba priests and priestesses become a *baba* (godfather) and *iya* (godmother). They perform the rituals and initiations and present offerings, but it's you, the devotee, who must learn to uplift yourself. Aṣe!

Aboru, Aboye, Aboṣiṣe

May the offerings be carried

May the offerings be accepted

May the offerings set divine forces in motion.

APPENDIX

Religious Phrases of the Yoruba

Yoruba	English Translation
Ohun ori wa se Ko ma ni s alai se eo	What ori comes to fulfill, It cannot but fulfill it.
Aye l'oja, orun n'ile	The world is a marketplace. The spirit world is home.
Ohun gbogbo ti a ba se laye la ookunle re lorun	That which we do on earth, we shall account for kneeling in heaven.
Ebo fin, Eru da	The offerings are accepted, evil forces depart. (This is stated after the ebo or offering has been completed.)
Ojo o buru, ebon nii gbe ni o	In days of turbulence, it is ebo that saves.
Ṣ otito ṣ ododo ṣ oora ma ṣ ika	Perform truth, perform righteousness, perform kindness, avoid cruelty.
Ni nyin awon awo, awon awo nyin sa	She/he was praising the diviners, the diviners were praising oriṣa.
Dide dide lalafia	Arise, arise, in peace.
Iṣe Olorun tobi	God's work is great and mighty.
Ka maa woriṣa	Let us keep looking to the oriṣa.
Mo fe bo	I want to worship.
Orunmila eleri ipin ibekeji Olodumare	Orunmila, witness of fate second to the Creator.

B'ao ku iṣe o tan	When there's life, there's hope.
Abo ru, Abo ye, Abo ṣiṣe	May the offerings be carried, may the offerings be accepted, may the offerings bring about change. (Salutation to babalawos by all Yoruba traditionalists)
Bi owe, bi owe, ru Ifa soro	Like proverbs, like proverbs, is how Ifa speaks.
Riru ebo ni i gbe ni airu ki i gbe eyan	It's the offerings of sacrifices that bring blessings. Neglect of sacrifices blesses no one.
Fun wa ni alaafia	Let us have peace.
Imo, ogbon, oye	Knowledge, wisdom, understanding.

GLOSSARY

A

Aba: the manifestation of aṣe into righteous human development

Aborisa: a devotee of oriṣa who has received the ilekes

Adimu: offerings made to one's ancestors and to the oriṣa

Adura: prayers

Agbon: coconut

Agere: container or vessel which holds the sacred palm nuts (ikin of Orunmila)

Ago: listen

Aiku: long life

Aiye: earth

Ajagun: angelic warriors comprised of Eṣu, Ogun, Oshoosi, Oṣun

Ajogun: malevolent forces intent on destroying humankind

Ajubona: religious teacher

Alaaṣe: the codes of ancestral conduct

Alafia: peace

Apetebi: wife of an Ifa priest (babalawo)

Ara: body

Arun: sickness

Asaro: meditation

Aṣe: essence of primal power and creative potential

Ate: mat

Awe: fasting, religious abstinence from food

Awo: those of the priestly order

Ayanmo: destiny

B

Baba: father

Baba mi: my father

Babalawo: father of mysteries

Babal'oriṣa: priest of any one of the various sects of oriṣa
    worship

Babarugbo: old man

Bata: sacred drums of oriṣa worship (New World)

Bembe: communal worship as tribute to the Oriṣa (New World)

Beni: all is well; yes

C

Candomble: Yoruba religion combined with Catholicism as
    practiced in South America

D

Dida obi: cast obi for

Dide: arise

Difa fun: cast Ifa for

Dojude: darkness

E

Ebo: offerings to one's ancestors or to the orisas

Efun: white chalklike substance taken from the earth for religious consecration

Egun: ancestor

Egungun: society of priests who possess the spirits of the deceased

Elegun: those who are mounted/possessed by the orisa

Elehan/Isese/Ocha: period of three to seven days taken for priesthood initiation

Emi: the spiritual essence of a person's breath or being

Epo: palm oil

Eran: meat, animals

Ere orisa: images, statues, physical forms of the orisas

Ese: verse of the Ifa corpus

Etutu: ritual

Ewe: herbs and plants

Ewo: restriction, taboos

Ewure: she-goat

Eyele: pigeon

F

Fun: to give

Fun Fun: white

G

Gbogbo: all

Gelede: society that reconciles the differences between humans
and witches

I

Ibeji: twins

Ibi: to avert; aversion of misfortune

Ifa: the cosmic intelligence of Yoruba cultural expression

Ifunpa: amulet

Igbodu: hut constructed during babalawo initiations

Ijuba: the paying of homage or reverence

Ikin: sacred palm nuts used by the babalawo in worship and
divination

Ikoode: red parrot feather tied to the initiate's head during priestly initiation

Iku: death

Ile: house, temple

Ile-Ife: holy city of the Yoruba religion

Ilekes: spiritual beads consecrated to the oriṣa and presented to novices ceremoniously

Imo: knowledge

Imule: oath

Ire: blessings, good fortune

Irosun: camwood

Ita: divination at initiations performed on the third day

Itan: historical and mythological narratives described in the Ifa corpus

Itefa: the ritual ceremony of initiating the Ifa devotee to actual babalawo

Iwa-pele: balanced character

Iya: mother

Iyalawo: female counter of babalawo

Iyal'oriṣa: priestess of any one of the various sects of oriṣa worship

Iyawo: initiate into the priestly realm; wife of the oriṣa

Iyerosun: special powder used by the babalawo to mark the Odu on the Opon-Ifa

J

Jinle: deep (as in thought or expression)

K

Kekere: small, little

Kiki: moral of a verse or story

L

Lucumi: Yoruba religion combined with Spanish Catholicism in Cuba

M

Mariwo: palm fonds

Meji: two or twice

Merindilogun: sixteen cowrie shells used by priest and priestesses for Ifa divination

Modupe: I give thanks

Mojuba: I give homage

O

Oba: chief; king

Obe: knife

obi abata: kola nuts divided in four parts used for divination

Odabo: goodbye

Odu: sixteen heavenly disciples named by Orunmila as the epitome of Yoruba culture and religion

Ofo: loss

Oju Odu: the first sixteen Odu meji of the babalawo

Ojubo: sacred shrine room for orişa worship

Olodumare/Olorun: God

Ologberi: the uninitiated

Oloogun: medicine healers of the Yoruba

Olori ebi: religious head of the family or social function

O'lorişa: male and female priests

Omi: water

Omiero: herbal solution used for spiritual baths and consecration of religious objects

Omo: child

Omo-aiye: malevolent human beings

Omo Odu: the 240 combinations of different Odu casts

Ona: road

Onifa: worshippers of Orunmila

Onile: Earth goddess

Onje: food, meals

Opele: the divining chain of the babalawo

Opon Ifa: round or rectangular wooden tray used by babalawo to divine

Oriki: praise songs and chants to the orisa

Orin: songs to the orisa

Orisa/Orisa: angelic emanations of the Creator manifesting through nature

Orita: crossroads

Orun: sky; heaven

Orunmila: the prophet of the Yoruba religion

Ota: stones as the symbols of immortality

Oti: strong alcoholic drink

Owo: money; prosperity

S

Santeria: Yoruba religion combined with Spanish Catholicism

Siju: light; open

Suuru: patience

T

Tutari: incense

Tutu: cool

V

Vodun: West African term meaning God; Yoruba and French Catholicism combined in Haiti

Y

Yoruba: ethnic group and culture of African origin

NOTES

Introduction

1. Isha Schwaller de Lubicz, *Her-Bak: Egyptian Initiate* (Rochester, VT: Inner Traditions, 1978), 369.

2. Omosade Awolalu, *Yoruba Beliefs and Sacrificial Rites* (White Plains, NY: Longman Group, 1979), 3.

3. Sophy Burnham, *A Book of Angels* (New York: Ballantine Books, 1990), 82.

4. *A Book of Angels*, 140.

Chapter 1: The Yoruba History

1. Basil Davidson, *The Lost Cities of Africa* (Boston: Little, Brown & Co, 1959), p. 60

2. *The Lost Cities of Africa*, p. 60.

3. Michael Omoleya, Certificate History of Nigeria (London & Lagos: Longman Group, 1986), p. 15.

4. Chei.k Anta Dio, *Precolonial Black Africa* (Trenton, NJ: Africa World Press, co-published with Lawrence Hill, 1992), p. 216.

5. On wu biko, KBC, *History of West Africa A.D. 1000–1800* (Onitsha, Nigeria: Africana-FEP Publisher, 1967),.

6. *History of West Africa*, 136.

7. Maureen Warner-Lewis, *Guinea's Other Suns* (Dover, MA: The Majority Press, 1991), 1.

8. *Guinea's Other Suns*, 51.

9. Robert Farris Thompson, *Flash of the Spirit* (New York: Vintage Books, 1984), xv.

Chapter 3: The Orisa

1. Isha Schwaller de Lubicz, *Her-Bak: Egyptian Initiate* (Rochester, VT: Inner Traditions, 1982), 27.

2. S. Popoola, "Life: Its Purpose and Hereafter" in *Orunmila,* Issue 3 (June 1987), 13.

3. "Life: Its Purpose and Hereafter," 15.

4. Omosade Awolalu, *Yoruba Beliefs and Sacrificial Rites* (White Plains, NY: Longman Group, 1979), 29.

5. *Yoruba Beliefs and Sacrificial Rites,* 30.

6. George Simpson, *Yoruba Religions and Medicines of Ibadan* (Ibadan University Press, 1980), 3.

7. M. Duko, "God & Godling's in African Ontology" in *Orunmila,* Issue 5 (June 1990), 49.

8. Information regarding the chakras is adapted from Harish Johari's *Chakras: Energy Centers of Transformation* (Rochester, VT: Inner Traditions, 1987).

9. Muhammad Ali, *The Muslim Prayer Book* (Ahmaduiyya, 1938), 11–14.

10. Omosade Awolalu, *Yoruba Beliefs and Sacrificial Rites* (White Plains, NY: Longman Group, 1979), 114.

11. Margaret Thompson Drewal, *Yoruba Ritual: Performers, Plays, Agency* (Bloomington: Indiana University Press, 1992), 23.

12. See: John Mason's *Orin Orisa: Songs for Selected Heads* (Yoruba Theological Archministry, 1992). The Yoruba religious songs are part of the New World Orisa tradition. You may find some of these songs in orisa dance classes or at your local music store in the international section.

13. Adapted from Bolaji Idowu's *Olodumare: God in Yoruba Belief* (London: Longmans, Green, 1961).

14. Kofi Opoku, *West African Traditional Religion* (FEP International Private Limited, 1978), 53.

15. *West African Traditional Religion,* 53.

Chapter 4: Divination, Sacrifice, Initiations

1. *Agbon* is the Yoruba term for coconut, yet when used for religious purposes in the New World, the term *obi* is applied. This reflects the transferences of usage, not a misnaming of object.

2. Mircae Eliade, *From Primitive to Zen* (New York: Harper & Row, 1967).

3. Wande Abimbola, *Ifa: An Exposition of Ifa Literary Corpus* (Oxford: Oxford University Press, 1976), 18.

4. John S. Mbiti, *Introduction to African Religion* (Portsmouth, NH: Heinemann, 1975), 126.

5. *Introduction to African Religion,* 126.

BIBLIOGRAPHY

Abimbola, Wande. *Ifa*. Oxford: Oxford University Press, 1976.

———. *Sixteen Great Poems of Ifa*. Unesco and Abimbola, 1975.

Ali, Muhammad. *The Muslim Prayer Book*. Ahmadiyya, 1938.

Apter, Andrew. *Black Critics and Kings*. Chicago: University of Chicago Press, 1992.

Awolalu, J. Omasade. *Yoruba Beliefs and Sacrificial Rites*. White Plains, NY: Longman Group, 1979.

Bascom, William. *Ifa Divination*. Bloomington: Indiana University Press, 1991.

———. *The Yoruba of Southwestern Nigeria*. Prospect Heights, IL: Waveland Press, 1969.

Burnham, Sophy. *A Book of Angels*. New York: Ballantine Books, 1990.

Cortes, Enrique. *Secretos del Oriata de la Religion Yoruba*. Vilaragut Articulos Religiosos Com, 1980.

Davidson, Basil. *The Lost Cities of Africa*. Boston: Little, Brown, 1988.

De Lubicz, Isha Schwaller. *Her Bak: Egyptian Initiate*. Rochester, VT: Inner Traditions, 1982.

Diallo, Yaya, and Mitchell Hall. *The Healing Drum*. Rochester, VT: Destiny Books, 1989.

Diop, Cheik Anta. *Precolonial Black Africa*. Trenton, NJ: Africa World Press, co-published with Lawrence Hill, 1992.

Drewal, Henry, and John Pemberton III. *Yoruba: Nine Centuries of African Art and Thought*. New York: The Center for African Art in association with Harry N. Abrams, 1989.

Drewal, Margaret Thompson. *Yoruba Ritual*. Bloomington: Indiana University Press, 1992.

Eliade, Mircea. *From Primitives to Zen*. New York: Harper & Row, 1967.

Epega, Afolabi. *Obi: The Mystical Oracle of Obi Divination*. Bronx, NY: Imole Oluwa Institute, 1985.

Fasade, Olaoluwa. *The Herbs of Orişa*. Iwa's Publishing, 1991.

Gideons Holy Bible.

Graves, Kersey. *The Worlds Sixteen Crucified Saviors*. San Diego, CA. Truth Seeker, 1991.

Heinerman, John. *Herbal Dynamics*. Root of Life, 1982.

Ibie, Cromwell Osamoro. *Ifism: The Complete Work of Orunmila*. Hong Kong: Design Printing, 1986.

Idowu, Bolaji. *Olodumare: God in Yoruba Belief*. London: Longmans, Green, 1961.

Johnson, Samuel. *The History of the Yorubas: From the Earliest Times to the Beginning of the British Protectorate*. New York: Routledge, 1971. Reprint of the 1921 edition.

Karenga, Maulana. *The Husia*. Los Angeles: Kawaida Publications, 1984.

Lawson, E. Thomas. *Religions of Africa*. San Francisco: Harper & Row, 1985.

Leslau, Charlotte and Wolf. *African Proverbs*. White Plains, NY: Peter Pauper Press, 1962.

Mason, John. *Four New World Yoruba Rituals*. Yoruba Theological Archministry, 1985.

———. *Orin Orişa: Songs for Selected Heads*. Yoruba Theological Archministry, 1992.

Mbiti, John S. *Introduction to African Religion*. Portsmouth, NH: Heinemann, 1975.

McClelland, E. *The Cult of Ifa Among the Yoruba*. Anchor Press, 1982.

Minick, Michael. *The Wisdom of Kung Fu*. New York: William Morrow and Company, 1974.

Omolewa, Michael. *Certificate History of Nigeria*. London: Longman Group, 1986.

Onwubiko, KBC. *History of West Africa*. Ontisha, Nigeria: Africana-FEP Publisher, 1967.

Opoku, Kofi Asare. *West African Traditional Religion*. FEP International Private, 1978.

Orunmila Magazine, Lagos, Nigeria: Orunmila Youngsters International.

Simpson, George E. *Yoruba Religion & Medicine in Ibadan*. Ibadan University Press, 1980.

Thompson, Robert Farris. *Flash of Spirit*. New York: Vintage Books, 1984.

Warner-Lewis, Maureen. *Guinea's Other Suns*. Dover, MA: Majority Press,1991.

Williams, Geoffrey. *African Designs from Traditional Sources*. New York: Dover Publications, 1971.

Witte, Hans. *Earth and the Ancestors: Ogboni Iconography*. Amsterdam: Gallery Balolu, 1988.

————. *Ifa and Esu*. Holland: Kunsthandel, Luttik, 1984.

Yusef Ali, Abdullah. *The Holy Quran*. Islamic Propagation Center International, 1946.

INDEX

PHOTO BY MANSA K. MUSSA

About the Author

OLOYE "BABA" IFA KARADE is one of the foremost pioneers of the Yoruba tradition in the United States. He has traveled to Nigeria, West Africa, Brazil, Trinidad, Puerto Rico, the Netherlands, and throughout the United States gathering and journaling on his experiences, data, revelations, and insights. He is the author of *Ojise, Messenger of the Yoruba Tradition* and several other related texts. Baba Ifa Karade served as a lecturer and panelist on oriṣa studies at various universities and conferences worldwide. He's been on radio and online radio web programs and featured in magazines and newspapers. He's a retired secondary school teacher and currently an adjunct professor of English at Essex County College in Newark, New Jersey. In 2003, he was presented with a Lifetime Achievement Award for his outstanding work in the Ifa community. In 2011, an archive was established in his name. He continues to write fiction and nonfiction books and articles based on the Ifa/Yoruba religion and spirituality.

To Our Readers

Weiser Books, an imprint of Red Wheel/Weiser, publishes books across the entire spectrum of occult, esoteric, speculative, and New Age subjects. Our mission is to publish quality books that will make a difference in people's lives without advocating any one particular path or field of study. We value the integrity, originality, and depth of knowledge of our authors.

Our readers are our most important resource, and we appreciate your input, suggestions, and ideas about what you would like to see published.

Visit our website at *www.redwheelweiser.com* to learn about our upcoming books and free downloads and be sure to go to *www.redwheelweiser.cosm/newsletter* to sign up for newsletters and exclusive offers.

You can also contact us at *info@rwwbooks.com* or at

Red Wheel/Weiser, LLC
65 Parker Street, Suite 7
Newburyport, MA 01950

Also in Weiser Classics

The Book of Lies
by Aleister Crowley, with an introduction
by Richard Kaczynski

Futhark: A Handbook of Rune Magic (Revised Edition)
by Edred Thorsson

*The Herbal Alchemist's Kitchen: A Complete Guide
to Magickal Herbs and How to Use Them*
by Karen Harrison, with a foreword by
Arin Murphy-Hiscock

*Psychic Self-Defense: The Definitive Manual for Protecting
Yourself Against Paranormal Attack*
by Dion Fortune, with a foreword by Mary K. Greer

Yoga Sutras of Patanjali
by Mukunda Stiles, with a foreword by Mark Whitwell